Teaching Oregon Native Languages

T0338165

Teaching Oregon Native Languages

Edited by Joan Gross

**Oregon State
University Press
Corvallis**

To all the teachers and learners of lesser-known languages

Photo on pages i and iii by Judy Blankenship, courtesy of Northwest Regional Educational Laboratory.

The paper in this book meets the guidelines for permanence and durability of the Committee on Production Guidelines for Book Longevity of the Council on Library Resources and the minimum requirements of the American National Standard for Permanence of Paper for Printed Library Materials Z39.48-1984.

Library of Congress Cataloging-in-Publication Data
Teaching Oregon native languages / edited by Joan Gross.
    p. cm.
  Includes bibliographical references and index.
  ISBN 978-0-87071-193-0 (alk. paper)
    1. Indians of North America—Oregon—Languages--Study and teaching. 2. Languages—Oregon—Study and teaching. I. Gross, Joan.
  PM501.O7T43 2007
  497.071--dc22

                                                      2007034944

Oregon State University Press
121 The Valley Library
Corvallis OR 97331
541-737-3166 • fax 541-737-3170
http://oregonstate.edu/dept/press

Contents

Acknowledgements

This book grew out of an interest group at Oregon State University that came together out of a common concern with Native languages in the state of Oregon. Joseph Krause and Armelle Hofer were important members of this group, along with Joan Gross, Deanna Kingston, and Juan Trujillo. Allison Davis-White Eyes in the Indian Education office was always there for support. We had been approached by Myra Johnson, director of the Warm Springs language program, and later by Stephanie Ohles of the Klamath Tribes language program, for help with teaching methodology. Together we put on two conferences entitled "Speaking to the Seventh Generation" in 2002 and 2003, with the help of the departments of Anthropology and Foreign Languages and the generous funding of Spirit Mountain Community Fund. In so doing, we got to know Native language workers in the state and were able to provide a forum in which they could interact with Native scholars of language revitalization (Stephen Greymorning, Phil Cash Cash, Ofelia Zepeda and Kathy Sikorski) as well as a well-known native archivist (Alyce Sadongei) and the actress Lucy Tulugarjuk, who presented the prize-winning Inuit-language film, *The Fast Runner*. Through these interactions, we came to know of the possibilities for Native languages and also the obstacles to maintaining strong Native language programs in the state. One of the obstacles is the lack of knowledge concerning Native American languages and the revitalization movement in the state, and so the idea for this book was born.

Four students helped the editor with the interviews that were conducted on reservations around the state in the spring and summer of 2004 and their subsequent transcription: Erin Haynes, Emily Riley, Katora Ruiz, and Fidelia Twenge-Jinings. Haines and Twenge-Jinings have continued working with Oregon languages in their graduate studies at UC Berkeley and Portland State University respectively. Riley has assisted with a variety of tasks associated with putting this book together: printing, mailing, formatting, etc.

This book would not have been possible without the numerous people working in Native language programs and studying Native languages who took the time to answer our questions and help us understand the delights and the challenges in learning and teaching these precious languages. We list most of their names below. Others who were equally generous with their time preferred that their names not be used and we have respected their wishes.

Manny P. Calapoo, Anna Clements, Kathy Cole, Karen Crutcher, R. Jane Crutcher, Rose Curtis, Andrew Dave, Randolph "Bobby" David, Judith Fernandez, Jimmy Freeman, Evan Gardner, Janice George-Hill, Jerry Hall, Fred Hill, Derek Hinkey, David Hinkey, Jackie Jackson, Wendell Jim, Myra Johnson, Radine Johnson, Rosie Johnson, Tony Johnson, Karla Kalama, Ruth Lewis, Bobbie Mercier, Adeline Miller, Patricia Miller, Malissa Minthorn, Tina Montoya, Thomas Morning Owl, Gloria Muñiz, Jess Nowland, Stephanie Ohles, Mildred Quaempts, Inez Reeves, Leslie Riggs, Arlita Rhoan, Noel Rude, Louis Scott, Willy Sigo, Randee Sheppard, Lawrence J. Squiemphen, Jhanna Stutzman-Fry, Tim Thornes, Gilbert Towner, Shirley Tufti, Phyllis Walker, Sonny Warren Ryan and Dallas Winishut

It goes without saying that we thank our families for their understanding while we worked on our respective parts of this book. Gross wants to especially thank her son, Stanley, who accompanied the interviewing team when he was thirteen, and was complimented on being a very good listener.

Language Notes

As with all unstandardized languages, the spelling of the names of Oregon Native languages varies. In addition, the same language is often referred to by different names and the names in English do not match the names in the Native language. Here are some of the variations you might come across.

Chinook Jargon, Chinuk Wawa, Chinook Pidgin, Tsinuk Wawa
Coos, Miluk, Hanis
Lukiamute, Luckamiut, Lakmayut, Lakmiyuk
Molala, Molale, Molalla, Mollala, Molele
Nez Perce, Nez Percé, Nimipu, Nee me poo
Northern Paiute, Numu
Tualatin, Twalatin
Tututni, Tootooten, Tututen
Tolowa, Smith River, Southwest Coast Athapaskan (In "Athapaskan," the "th" can alternate with "t"; the "p" with "b" and the "k" with "c.")
Umatilla, Immatillam, Columbia River Sahaptin
Wasco, Was'qu, Kiksht, Wasco-Wishram, Upper Chinook
Klamath, ?ewksiknii
Walla Walla, Walulapum, Northeast Sahaptin
Warm Springs, Ichishkiin, Tenino, Sahaptin

Note that Warm Springs, Umatilla, Walla Walla, and Yakima (spoken in Washington) may all be referred to as "Sahaptin." Of these, Walla Walla is the most unlike the other three and thus is harder to understand. Even though speakers of Umatilla and Warm Springs can communicate with each other, we were told of several misunderstandings that occurred between the two dialects. The languages that are being revitalized in the state of Oregon are classified by linguists as belonging to three large groupings of languages, called phyla: Aztec-Tanoan, Na-Dene, and Penutian.

Introduction

The United States of America began as a multilingual settler colony, but before European conquest multiple languages had interacted with each other within what are now the borders of the United States. A concerted effort to make the United States into a monolingual country began in the nineteenth century, and was quite successful. It began with the attempt to eradicate Native American languages and continued with the abandonment of other immigrant languages, except for English. Preference for English speakers was even encoded into immigration law. Despite the myth of a British heritage, in 1983 less than 30 percent of Americans could trace a significant portion of their ancestry to England and the percentage is still lower today.[1] Through the implementation of policy and the shaping of new American ideas about language, the country evolved into one of the most monolingual nations of the post-industrial world. The USA has squandered its linguistic resources to an even greater extent than it has squandered natural resources. The consequences of this ideology have not been made clear to the majority of Americans. On an international level, the country's capacity for intelligence gathering and diplomacy would be far greater if our linguistic resources were developed. On a national level, an acceptance of multilingualism would lead to more respect for one another, more flexibility in ways of perceiving the world, and ultimately, a more deeply rooted democracy.

This book addresses only one part of the United States, the state of Oregon, and one group of Oregon's languages, Native American, because this story has not been told. It begins with a history of what happened to Native Americans in the state because when we ignore history, we cannot fully understand the present. We might even say that the U.S. population has been forced to forget its multilingual past. Even before the English-Only movement got started in the 1980s, English-only media and popular culture developed the idea that everyone had always spoken English here. Native Americans in T.V. and films only spoke a few words of simple English. This left viewers with the idea that Native Americans had simple thoughts, rather than emphasizing that they were communicating in a language they had learned as adults under conditions of coercion. The languages in which they were raised, the ones through which they learned their cultures, were carefully omitted from the scene. These languages presented a different worldview, one that was considered dangerous to the project of creating a nation-state based on principles

1

of uniformity, rather than diversity. The Native languages also did not fit with the project of extracting maximum monetary profit from natural resources.

We need only review the history of the Cherokees from southern Appalachia to realize the degree to which nineteenth-century "nation builders" were antagonistic to Native American languages. A Cherokee, Sequoyah, realized that the literacy of Euro-Americans was assisting them in their conquest. So he developed symbols that corresponded to vowels and consonant-vowel sequences in Cherokee. (This method of writing is known as a syllabary and is used in other languages as well, most notably Japanese.) Sequoyah's system was carefully crafted and the Cherokees were so committed to becoming literate that within a year the majority of the tribe's adults could read and write in Cherokee. In 1828, they established a printing press and began publishing a Cherokee newspaper. With the tools of literacy at their disposal, they translated U.S. law into Cherokee and mounted a judicial challenge to the 1830 Indian Removal Act. This is certainly democracy at its best; however it did not work in the Cherokees' favor. In spite of positive rulings from the U.S. Supreme Court, they were forced off their land and marched across the country to what later became Oklahoma. In 1835, the Georgia state government confiscated their printing press and destroyed it. Some Cherokees reestablished a press in Oklahoma, but when the U.S. government dissolved the Cherokee nation in 1907, the Cherokee press was once again confiscated. Children were forced to attend English-speaking schools, and literacy and fluency in the language declined.[2]

While Native American languages were the first target in the English crusade, imported languages other than English suffered as well. A clear case of language antagonism occurred in the U.S. Southwest, which had been settled by Spaniards two centuries prior to the arrival of Anglos. California was overrun by English speakers after the Gold Rush and quickly attained statehood by 1850. In New Mexico, the situation was quite different. Anglos remained a minority there until after 1900. In 1902 a special Congressional committee recommended that statehood be postponed until the territory was sufficiently "Americanized." Desiring the increased self-government offered to states, people began shifting to English in the public realm. In 1874 69 percent of the public schools taught entirely in Spanish, but by 1911 Spanish was neglected completely in the schools.[3] In 1912, New Mexico was accepted for statehood.

In recent years, when multiculturalism has become a standard part of our curriculum and public image, languages are usually absent. It is very easy to leave a multicultural fair with the impression that all these cultures speak English, save for a few choice words, such as "Aloha!" "Ciao!" and "Bonjour!" The exclamation points that we often see after these foreign words of greeting stand in for the real emotion that is often lacking in staged cultural performances. These performances are organized for easy consumption by an audience that has only a short amount of time to spend learning a few facts about a different culture. Learning a language requires a far more serious commitment, one that is not highly valued in the society that we have created. This stands in contrast to the value placed by Native Oregonians on learning the languages of other cultural groups. Good relations with surrounding cultures ensured that a group would survive and it was understood that good relations were based on the ability to communicate with these neighboring groups.

Recent research shows that the human brain becomes more complex with the experience of acquiring a second language. The bilingual brain has a higher density of grey matter in the left inferior parietal cortex and the density is even greater among people who learned a second language before the age of five.[4] Why, then, is so little effort put into developing multilingualism in the U.S.? Other cultures have long recognized the cognitive advantages of being multilingual. A Central European saying is: "The more languages you speak the more times you are a human being." In South Africa they say, "If you want to know me, know my language." Multilingual areas of the world consider the mastery of multiple languages to be a fundamental part of one's education. Only in the United States can one receive the highest educational degrees, Ph.D., M.D., J.D., without knowing any language other than English.

The focus of this book is on the revitalization of Oregon's native languages. As you may surmise, this is not an easy task in a country that has fought to be monolingual. Revitalizing a language once natural transmission of the language has been broken is never easy, but when it must be done in a context of intransigent monolingualism, the task is even more difficult. We think that it is a task worth doing. We are writing this book to tell others what is involved, what has been done, and what can be done to assist in this effort.

Language revitalization refers to a process by which a language that has declined in a particular community is brought back into usage. Language decline refers to both a decline in the number of people who speak the language and a reduction in the number of domains in which the language is spoken. For instance, a language that used to be spoken in all areas of life but is now restricted to religious services has suffered a reduction in domains of use. Languages that were spoken by one's ancestors are called "heritage languages." Language revitalization efforts almost always take place within heritage language communities. It is important to distinguish between the revitalization of languages within a heritage community that has migrated to another place and left behind a vibrant community of speakers, and a heritage community that represents the last speakers of a particular language. The latter situation is what we will discuss in this book.

We think the primary reason language revitalization efforts should be supported is for the well-being of the speakers. It's difficult to argue against that. Humans are the most social of animals and we know that they are happier and healthier when they are respected. Colonial conquest that forced people to abandon their language and culture weighs heavily on many indigenous peoples throughout the world. Supporting them in their efforts to regain some of what was taken linguistically and culturally helps develop the mutual respect that is so necessary to a democratic society.

In addition to increasing human capital in heritage language communities, the preservation of lesser-known languages adds to the knowledge base of the human race in several different ways. Language is the most amazing creation of the human species, specifically because it is what creates us as humans. It is through language that we learn our culture and through language that all our other accomplishments have been nurtured. Language systems around the world show both similarities and differences at levels of phonology, morphology, syntax, semantics, and pragmatics. They encode nature and history. When whole languages drop out of the mix, it creates a gap in our knowledge base. We hear almost daily about the tragedy of endangered and extinct animal species, but until recently no one seemed to care that at least half of the world's approximately six thousand languages are on the path to extinction. Last speakers of languages die regularly with little recognition.

A recent joint effort to support the documentation of endangered languages by the National Science Foundation, the National Endowment for the Humanities, and the Smithsonian Institution emphasizes the importance of language preservation for scientists and scholars. The Call for Proposals for the Documenting Endangered Languages Initiative states:

• Each endangered language embodies unique local knowledge of the cultures and natural systems in the region in which it is spoken.

• These languages are among the few sources of evidence for filling in the record of the human past.

• The great variety of these languages represents a vast, largely unmapped terrain on which linguists, cognitive scientists, and philosophers can chart the full capabilities—and limits—of the human mind.

It is time for scholars and Native communities to band together to preserve and revitalize these languages for the good of generations to come. It is with this goal in mind that we present this book: a tool to educate the general public and, especially, policy makers and educators about the history and transmission of Oregon's native languages. In it, we explore policies that help and hinder the revitalization of these languages; we explain the creation and use of Native Oregon language archives; and we demonstrate how to use the latest language-teaching methodologies to support heritage-language revitalization. As the title of the book clearly states, the focus is on teaching these languages. It is not a book on genetic links between the languages or on the grammatical structure of any single language. It does not focus exclusively on any particular Native language program in the state, but elucidates the challenges that all of them face. It is a book firmly grounded in academic research in linguistics, anthropology, and language pedagogy, but is presented in a way that is accessible to a general population. Our hope is that it will be used in courses throughout the state, answering the request from Oregon's tribes that native issues be included in the education of all Oregonians. We have a particular interest in reaching the educators of the next generation of Oregonians and we hope that Native peoples comprise an increasing number of these educators. Schools played a major role in the destruction of local languages. Now it is time for them to play a positive role. Language revitalization projects are difficult enough when whole communities are supporting them. When most of the citizens of a state do not even know that endangered languages exist close by, the task is overwhelming.

Gross begins chapter one by looking at the state of languages in Oregon from the time of Euro-American contact through the establishment of English monolingualism, paying attention to the development of Chinook Jargon. She documents a shift to a monolingual ideology by mining references to language from old reports and places Oregon within the context of colonialism and developing American national policy. The effects of new diseases and the reservation system on the maintenance of Native languages are explored. Since education is the social institution that most clearly influences language attitudes, this chapter focuses on the formation of Indian day schools and boarding schools and the policies aimed at breaking the natural transmission of Native languages.

Chapter two, based largely on interviews with teachers and students in Native language programs, picks up at the point when Native people realized that their languages must be consciously taught if they are to survive. Gross addresses the topic from a more personal angle in this chapter. Stories give us insight into how languages were lost and maintained over the lifetimes of individuals and families. Language workers describe the challenges of teaching languages today.

In chapter three Haynes examines the role of education policy in the language-revitalization efforts made by Oregon tribes. Language policy in the United States has been concentrated especially in the field of education, where policy decisions affect how and when languages can be taught, who can teach them, and which languages are appropriate for instruction. Haines discusses the cultural values and attitudes that lead to the creation of educational practices and policies and their effects on Native American students. She summarizes legislation at both the federal and state level that has had direct consequences for Oregon's Native language programs, including the Native American Languages Act, the No Child Left Behind Act, Oregon Senate Bill 690, and other bills and official statements. She ends with a discussion of English-only legislation, which threatens to undermine the toehold that Native languages have gained in public schools.

Kingston and Lewis trace the history of research on Oregon Native languages in chapter four. Early language materials were collected under colonial conditions and ended up far from where they were collected. The authors underline the importance of past research and archives, despite their colonial foundation, in creating curricula for languages that are no longer widely spoken. Funding for tribal archives has been scarce, but recent efforts by tribal members have led to the repatriation of archival materials to local tribes and increased collaboration with state libraries. Internet resources are always growing and the authors cite some of the most important Web sites.

In chapter five, Trujillo discusses best practices in language teaching that are firmly grounded in academic research on the nature of language and language learning. After tracing the history of language-teaching trends in the U.S., he advocates a cultural approach focused on communication in real situations. Trujillo suggests ways in which tribal language teachers can use the National Standards for Foreign Language Learning and proposes a sixth standard based on the consciousness of systems of oppression and the commitment to social equity.

Chapter One

Forging a Monolingual Country

Joan Gross

Introduction

What became the state of Oregon, an area stretching south from the Columbia Gorge to the Siskiyous, and east from the Pacific over the Coastal Range and Cascades to the High Desert, was a land of many languages, each one encoding information about the land and how to survive on it. Linguistic anthropologist Dell Hymes estimates that before Europeans landed in Oregon eighteen very different languages were represented in the state.[1] Other estimates go up to twenty-five. The first Europeans to arrive spoke different dialects of Russian, Spanish, and French before English speakers came on the scene. Yet today close to 90 percent of the state's population speaks only English at home.

Our focus is on languages within the state of Oregon. Borders around languages are notoriously difficult to draw and they change over time. We chose the state borders because the state defines a regional level of government where language and school policies are set. It represents a political arena within which social activism can occur. At the same time, we recognize that the state forms a very artificial border *vis à vis* Native languages. Sahaptin and Chinuk Wawa teachers collaborate with individuals in Washington; Nez Perce teachers have a stronger base in Idaho; and Northern Paiute teachers borrow curricular materials from Nevada, as do Tolowa teachers from California. All the Northwest language activists have benefited from language revitalization efforts in the southwestern U.S., Hawaii, and even other countries, especially New Zealand.

The linguistic landscape of Oregon during the early years of Euro-American colonialism can be partially reconstructed based on early documents and on what we know from other studies of languages in contact. This rich and complex assortment of languages did not last Euro-American colonization. The natural transmission of language and culture from older generations to younger generations was broken in three major ways. Death due to introduced diseases dealt a terrible blow to Native speech communities. Forcing people off their traditional lands and onto reservations created further cultural and linguistic disruption. The introduction of residential boarding schools completed the assault on the natural transmission of Oregon's Native languages.

Multilingualism and Lingua Francas

The various languages of Oregon belong to language families as different from each other as English is from Arabic: Athabaskan, Salishan, Shastan, Uto-Aztecan, and a number of families that have been roughly grouped into the Penutian phylum (Chinookan, Kalapuyan-Takelman, Sahaptian, Lutuamian, Molallan, Cayusan, Yakonan, Siuslawan, Coosan). Each of these families consisted of several languages, and each language of several spoken dialects. Even within what might be called the same dialect, each village probably had its own subdialect, differing from the neighboring village in the way certain sounds were pronounced and a few vocabulary words. A chain of related dialects would form a language area as has been documented in other places in the world.

Linguists calculate the relatedness of languages in the same way that natural scientists classify plants and animals. Sub dialects are grouped into dialects, which are grouped into languages, which are grouped into families, which are grouped into phyla. However, in reality, the classification of languages is more complex because languages exist in the social world and people have clear opinions about their nature. For example, one of the criteria on which relatedness is based is intelligibility: do the speakers of dialect A understand the speakers of dialect B? However, this is not a straightforward question. There are documented cases of people who used to "understand" each other rather suddenly claiming not to under new political circumstances, for instance when both groups claim the same piece of land. Another complication is the labeling of some speech varieties as "dialects" and others as "languages." A well-known saying in linguistic circles is "A language is a dialect with an army and a navy." Translating this saying into the Native American context, we might say that a language is a dialect with an anthropologist and a linguist. The major difference between what we call a "dialect" or a "language" falls outside the realm of linguistics and into the realm of social power. In general, as people recognize a particular group of people as culturally distinct from others, their language is also regarded as being more distinct. It is probably more accurate to think about the spoken resources of the world as bundles of dialects, some of which have far more power in the world.

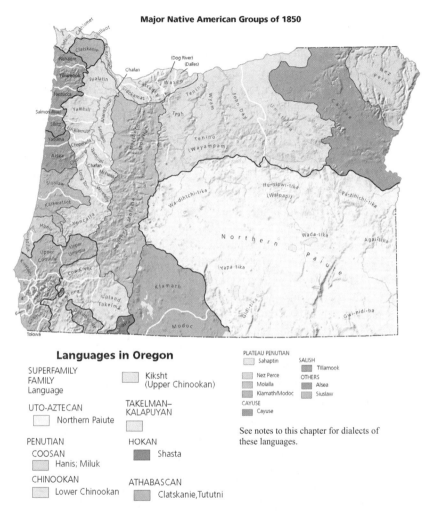

Major Native American Groups of 1850

Languages in Oregon

SUPERFAMILY
FAMILY
Language

UTO-AZTECAN
  Northern Paiute

PENUTIAN
COOSAN
  Hanis; Miluk

CHINOOKAN
  Lower Chinookan

Kiksht
(Upper Chinookan)

TAKELMAN–
KALAPUYAN

HOKAN
  Shasta

ATHABASCAN
  Clatskanie, Tututni

PLATEAU PENUTIAN
  Sahaptin

  Nez Perce
  Molalla
  Klamath/Modoc

CAYUSE
  Cayuse

SALISH
  Tillamook
OTHERS
  Alsea
  Siuslaw

See notes to this chapter for dialects of
these languages.

While linguists have grouped languages according to similar
syntactic and morphological features, speakers of Native languages
in Oregon were more likely to think of languages other than their
own as the language spoken by their father's mother or their second
cousin. Multilingualism appears to have been quite common within
Native Oregon families. From what we know, the speakers of the
various dialects in what became Oregon were not isolated from each
other, but formed part of extensive trading routes up and down the
coast, along the Columbia River, and even across the high desert.
So it would have been advantageous to marry people from different
linguistic groups in order to have translators in the family and familial
relations with other tribes. Having relatives across a wide area would
give one access to different kinds of resources at different times

of the year. These interrelationships between speakers of different languages led to a high degree of multilingualism.

The multilingualism of the Native Northwest was noted by linguists who arrived in the early twentieth century. Edward Sapir's Wishram informant Pete McGuff also spoke fluent Klickitat.[2] Louis Kenoyer spoke both Yamhill and Tualatin.[3] Annie Miner Peterson spoke both the Hanis and Miluk dialects of Coos. Leo Frachtenburg had elicited Hanis from her decades earlier without ever finding out that she spoke Miluk too. In 1933, when Melville Jacobs went back to work with her, he found that only she "of all Coos Bay survivors" knew Miluk well enough to speak it.[4] Haruo Aoki wrote about the high degree of multilingualism among the Nez Perce and the Interior Salish and noted several examples from surrounding tribes of myth tellers using different languages to represent different mythological characters.[5] Let us remember that most of the Native language speakers who tediously worked with early linguists and anthropologists to record words, paradigms, and stories in their languages spoke Chinook Jargon (see below) and English as well. If they didn't, there were other Natives who translated between languages. Jacobs wrote to Franz Boas in 1934 suggesting that the trouble they often experienced trying to record the Native languages was not a matter of decaying Native speech as much as of spotty English skills possessed by their interpreters.[6] This tells us that, as late as the 1930s, English was still not the dominant language in many Indian families, though most Natives had learned enough to get by in it.

In addition to the high value placed on learning multiple Native languages, there was still a need for a means of communication in short-term encounters between speakers of different languages.[7] This need was filled by the creation of a trade language that came to be known as Chinook Jargon. By the time Lewis and Clark made their voyage down the Columbia, there is some evidence of a mixed language being spoken, but it most certainly stabilized into a pidgin language during the fur-trading period. John Jacob Astor established the Pacific Fur Company at the mouth of the Columbia in 1811 and many of his men were Canadians of French and Indian background. This particular ethnic mix continued to be an important element in the fur trade. By 1825, the Hudson's Bay Company had thirteen establishments and two hundred male employees in Oregon country; many of these were of mixed parentage themselves and many more married mixed-parentage or "full-blooded" Indian women. Indian wives had to live outside of the trading posts with their growing number of children, forming a semi-separate society. It was in this subsociety that Chinook Jargon probably developed into a viable means of communication in domains outside of trade.[8]

What began as a trade language with very limited vocabulary expanded into a pidgin and spread around the region. Both natives and Euro-Americans in the Northwest saw the advantage of this easily learned language. Pidgins have a simplified grammatical structure and are much easier to learn than historically rooted languages that have developed all sorts of unsystematic complexities over the years. People probably found that they could become somewhat proficient in Chinook Jargon in about six weeks of practice, whereas it would take several years to become relatively proficient in Chinook, for example. Because of this, Euro-Americans put much less effort into learning the historically rooted Native languages and learned Chinook Jargon instead. It served as a means of communication between speakers of different Native languages as well as between Natives and Euro-Americans. Gibbs wrote that there were few tribes between the 42nd and 57th parallel in which one could not find Chinook Jargon interpreters.[9] In their role as traders, the Klickitats appear to have spread the language to many southern Oregon groups. Languages that bridge communication gaps between speakers of different languages are known as lingua francas. Chinook Jargon quickly became the lingua franca of the Northwest.

We know that Euro-Americans developed a great interest in learning Chinook Jargon by the number of vocabulary lists that were published. Samuel Parker published a vocabulary list of just over one hundred Chinook Jargon words in 1838 and others followed on its heels. The first European nuns who arrived in the Willamette Valley in 1844 to teach the children growing up in this multicultural area used Chinook Jargon with their students. In 1863, a letter from C. M. Sawtelle, a teacher at the Grand Ronde Manual Labor School, stated that all twenty-three children were ignorant of the English language at first and the teachers had to resort to Chinook Jargon.[10] Several Chinook Jargon words drifted into Northwest frontier English. Words like "tyee" (chief), "skookum," (strong), "tillicum" (friend), "wawa" (talk), and "alki" (soon) were used to metaphorically claim identity with the region. An Oregon congressman in the 1880s talked about how General Sheridan and the translator, Nesmith, conversed in Chinook Jargon back in Washington, D.C. (Once, one of their telegrams was intercepted by the Secretary of War who, seeing the incomprehensible words, suspected that a plot was afoot.[11])

Many treaty negotiations were conducted through Chinook Jargon. Governor Isaac Stevens of the Washington Territory insisted that his official translator work only through Chinook Jargon when making treaties in 1854 and 1855, even though translators were available who knew both English and the regional Native languages.[12] Surveyor and ethnologist George Gibbs learned Chinook Jargon at Fort Astoria, then traveled as interpreter for the Redick McKee Expedition and helped negotiate the treaties with the California Indians in 1851. Later he served as interpreter for some of the Willamette Valley treaties.[13]

We should pause here and reflect on the process of translation/ interpretation. One interpreter would translate from English to Chinook Jargon and another would translate from Chinook Jargon to one of the native languages.[14] In this way, Chinook Jargon became a sort of filter language in conversations between speakers of European languages and speakers of Native American languages. We have to wonder whether Chinook Jargon at this point in time was equipped to clearly communicate some of the subtleties of the treaties. We also have to wonder about the match between the Chinook Jargon spoken by Euro-Americans and the Chinook Jargon spoken by Natives. Given the degree of social distance between the two groups and the vast differences in their native languages, it would seem likely that the dialects evolved along divergent paths.

George Gibbs postulated that Chinook Jargon originated after Euro-American contact. In his dictionary, published by the Smithsonian Institution in 1863, he presented the origins of Chinook Jargon words. He thought that this was necessary in part because mistakes were being made in the classification of Northwest Coast languages. The linguistic paradigm of the nineteenth century saw Native groups as bounded and separate, yet the same words were being used by the Nootkas (Nuu-Chah-Nulth) of Vancouver Island and the Chinooks of the Columbia. Gibbs pointed out that the words belonged to the trade language of Oregon, Chinook Jargon. The Chinook lived along the river year round, so their language was prevalent in the pidgin. Gibbs found twelve different source languages for the 490 Chinook Jargon words, but more than two hundred had their source in Chinook. Ninety-four had a French origin and sixty-seven, an English one. In Gibbs' view, the language had its origins in the 1770s, after Euro-Americans made contact with the Nuu-Chah-Nulth from the West Coast of Vancouver Island. They picked up words used in barter and "transplanted them with additions from the English, to the shores of Oregon."[15]

Gibbs presented a Eurocentric view, placing Euro-Americans at the center of the story as the prime movers in spreading Chinook Jargon down the coast. This view was understandable for its time and is supported by some linguistic evidence. Nevertheless, Gibbs also clearly stated that before Euro-American mariners arrived, "the coasting trade and warlike expeditions of the northern tribes, themselves a seafaring race, had opened up a partial understanding of each other's speech; for when, in 1792, Vancouver's officers visited Gray's Harbor, they found that the natives, though speaking a different language, understood many words of the Nootka."[16] This sounds like the type of cultural contact that could produce a simplified trade language onto which later European languages could have been grafted. The problem with sticking strictly to the written evidence is that it was all written by Euro-Americans for Euro-Americans during a time of intensive colonization.

Some linguists postulate that a pidgin language developed for the purposes of intertribal trade long before Euro-Americans arrived on the scene.[17] Without native writing systems, we have no direct evidence of this, but the situation described by early travelers and verified by archeology of the region is in alignment with the development of pidgins elsewhere in the world where people of multiple languages gather periodically for purposes of trade. This aptly describes the Columbia River during the salmon runs. Pidgins are formed when elements from several different languages come together in a simplified grammatical system with a limited vocabulary. Pidgins are notorious for replacing vocabulary with different languages, as one group of speakers loses and another gains power. This is called relexification. Recent work by Nez Perce linguist Phil Cash Cash traces the sources of Chinook Jargon vocabulary and finds that prior to 1860 almost all of it came from indigenous languages, but after 1860, when European colonization intensified, lexical additions from non-indigenous sources became dominant.[18] In the 1840s, Belgian nuns at French Prairie noted in their diaries that French expressions were starting to be added to Chinook Jargon. In the 1850s Gibbs found more French than English vocabulary, though indigenous languages were still dominant. By the time of Oregon statehood in 1859, when English had become the prestigious language, English was beginning to replace some of the French vocabulary.

Tony Johnson, who directs the Grand Ronde language program today, discovered that many of the French borrowings in Chinook Jargon are also used in Michif. Michif is a mixed language (based largely on Cree verbs and French nouns) that is spoken mainly in central Canada by descendants of French traders and Cree Indians who call themselves Métis. It was carried west by the Métis *voyageurs* who were so active in the fur trade. One Chinook Jargon word, *mitas*, was thought to be a Cree word, but in Cree it means pants, while it means leggings in both Chinook Jargon and Michif. This gives us a clue that the word was quite possibly brought in by Michif speakers. It seems quite reasonable, then, that the "French" nouns in Chinook Jargon could also have been brought in through Michif, rather than directly from French speakers.

When the first school opened at Fort Vancouver in 1832, the children spoke Cree, Nez Perce, Chinook, Klickitat, and other Indian languages, but they spoke to each other most likely in Chinook Jargon.[19] Horatio Hale collected information on Chinook Jargon at Fort Vancouver in 1841 and wrote that these children have Chinook Jargon as their mother tongue and "speak it with more readiness and perfection than any other."[20] Whereas their parents could resort to another language to communicate complex ideas, the children figured out how to formulate complex ideas in Chinook Jargon, creating what is called a creole language. As a pidgin morphs into a creole in the minds of children, the grammar of the language becomes more complicated and subtle and the vocabulary grows. What was a simplified, limited language becomes a full-fledged language capable of expressing a wide range of thoughts.

If creolization of Chinook Jargon took place among the multicultural families of the fur traders, it seems likely that Chinook Jargon might have also undergone creolization in the mixed Native households in western Oregon. When we think of the vast cultural disruption that stemmed from the decimation by disease and the forced concentration on western reservations of the remnants of tribes speaking many languages, creolization seems a likely result. On the Siletz and Grande Ronde reservations, speakers of Tillamook, Siletz, Upper and Lower Umpqua, Cow Creek, Galice-Applegate, Coquille, Tututni, Tolowa-Chetco, Clatsop, Kathlamet, Clackamas, Santiam, Mary's River Kalapuya, Yoncalla, Takelma, Latgawa, Yaquina, Alsea, Siuslaw, Miluk, Hanis, and others formed joint households. In addition, many of the French-Indian descendants of Hudson's Bay employees moved to reservations. French surnames such as Petit, Lachance, and Labonte are commonly found among Oregon Natives. Hawaiian Natives and Euro-Americans were also part of the mix on reservations, each adding their linguistic resources to Chinook Jargon. Eventually the native languages died out as people shifted to speaking Chinook Jargon. Tony Johnson discovered this when he was trying to elicit Chinook from elders in the 1980s and '90s. He kept asking for Chinook words and phrases and they kept giving him words and phrases in Chinook Jargon. Over time, unconscious decisions had been made to shift to this creole language, a symbol of the multiculturalism of the Pacific Northwest.

Chinook Jargon was not a unified code. First of all, there was the likely divergence between Chinook Jargon dialects spoken by Euro-Americans and those spoken by Natives. Native Oregon languages use a similar set of sounds, but a set that is very different from European languages. Since Chinook Jargon was first learned by adults who always brand new languages with the sounds of their native languages, the pronunciation of words would differ greatly between Natives and Euro-Americans. Furthermore, the social conditions were such that Chinook Jargon remained a pidgin learned by adults in the Euro-American community, while it became a more complex creole in the mixed Native environment.

Secondly, Chinook Jargon was spoken over a vast amount of territory; regional Chinook Jargon dialects developed, often incorporating lexical items from the local indigenous languages. Melville Jacobs wrote to Franz Boas in 1933 that the Chinook Jargon texts that Jacobs had collected came from a "peculiarly local, if not individual Jargon style." He went on to say, "the presence of variant Jargon styles or dialects imposes upon us an obligation to secure texts of some fullness from each of the regions where Jargon is spoken."[21] Thirdly, unstandardized oral languages like Chinook Jargon change more rapidly through time. People who learned the language when French was the prestige code probably had different forms of expression than those who learned it after English had become the prestige code. All these aspects of Chinook Jargon created great diversity within the language.

Speakers of the language prefer to call it "Chinuk Wawa" ("wawa" meaning "talk"). This deletes the confusing term "jargon," which has two different meanings in linguistics. It is used to refer to a pidgin before it has achieved any stabilization *and* it is used for a specialized vocabulary set that is not understood by the general public, like the words you need to know to become a lawyer or doctor. But perhaps the term "Chinook Jargon" should be preferred in reference to the variety of the pidgin language as it was developed by Euro-Americans. Tony Johnson reports that the phrases transcribed by Lewis and Clark are perfectly comprehensible to Chinuk Wawa speakers today, yet much of what he reads in later published vocabulary lists sounds quite foreign to them, indicating the dialect divergence postulated in the last paragraph. It is perfectly reasonable to expect that the population who had access to the power code of English would not develop the language in the same way that Natives would who needed it for a greater diversity of domains.

The development of Chinuk Wawa in the Northwest eventually took a toll on the indigenous languages, but English continued to grow in use and prestige. In its earlier pidgin form, Chinuk Wawa was only used in a few domains between fluent speakers of different languages, so it posed no threat to the indigenous languages. As it became a creole, however, it began being used in more and more domains and eventually pushed out other languages. This is a common occurrence in creole areas. As the creole gained in status *vis à vis* the indigenous languages, it still occupied the low status position *vis à vis* English. A similar situation developed in the American South and in Hawaii where low-status creole languages co-occurred with the prestige language, English. This mirrors the situation found in the Antilles today between Haitian Creole and standard French.

When the high-status language remains in contact with the creole, the creole becomes more like the standard until, eventually, it is perceived as being simply a low-status variety of the standard. This describes how African American Vernacular English and Hawaiian Pidgin English evolved. It is not out of line to suspect that a similar English variety developed here in the Northwest; a language that came to be seen as a regional variety of English, but which contained vestiges of Chinuk Wawa and other Native languages.

While we can spot linguistic patterns around the world, individual places have their own historical conditions that make them unique. For instance, the Northwest did not develop a plantation economy like the ones that characterized Hawaii and the American South. Native Americans were used for seasonal agricultural labor, but no laws were passed to make it illegal to teach them to read and write in English, as was the case with African Americans. Also, the local tribal structure and linguistic resources were not as unified as they were in Hawaii. In fact, where the linguistic groups were larger and more unified east of the Cascades, Chinuk Wawa did not hurry along the demise of other indigenous languages the way that it did in the western part of the state. Specific conditions concerning the size and relationships between cultural groups shaped the linguistic environment in Oregon. The multilingualism of the area made people receptive to adding a new language, be it Chinuk Wawa or English. Other conditions accelerated the shift to English, such as the decimation of the population through disease, the formation of reservations, and mandated boarding schools. The rest of the chapter is devoted to these topics.

Population Decimation

The first blow to native languages in Oregon arrived before major European incursions into the area. The coming of European diseases and diseases from other parts of the Americas brought by European travelers presaged the coming of Euro-American settlement in the Northwest. Robert Boyd outlines the waves of epidemics in the Northwest in his book, *The Coming of the Spirit of Pestilence,* which I follow closely here. Smallpox, malaria, tuberculosis, dysentery, and influenza, and various venereal diseases all took a great toll on tribal people of Oregon who had no immunity to them. Most of us have not experienced an epidemic that indiscriminately attacks a large percentage of our relatives, friends, and acquaintances. We might try to imagine what it would be like to be deathly ill and be surrounded by people too sick to care for us. The way that AIDS has taken hold in many places in Africa approximates the situation in the Northwest during the early contact years. Furthermore, not knowing why people were falling ill, nor how to best care for them, would put one's worldview in chaos.

It appears that smallpox must have been brought to the coast by the first Spanish explorers coming by sea in the 1770s, because a journal written aboard the ship *Columbia,* which stopped on the Oregon Coast near present-day Lincoln City in 1788, noted that some of their visitors were "much pitted with the small pox."[22] When Lewis and Clark arrived in 1805-6, they not only saw pock-marked people, but entire deserted villages along the Columbia and down the sea coast that they attributed to an earlier outbreak of smallpox.[23] Smallpox struck again a few years after Lewis and Clark left the area and again in 1836-37, killing an estimated twenty-five thousand and later thirty thousand West Coast people.

Smallpox was not the only menace. By the 1820s, tuberculosis had taken hold in western Oregon.[24] In the 1830s influenza hit Fort Vancouver, Fort Nez Perces, and the missions at Willamette and Waiilatpu, where the Cayuse had gathered to plant crops. Though Euro-Americans had had access to vaccines for a couple of years, it wasn't until 1837 that they began vaccinating Indians at Fort Vancouver and Fort Nez Perces.[25] Venereal disease was another result of contact. It was noted in Astoria in 1814 and subsequent sterility, miscarriages, and stillbirths caused a birth decline that was apparent in the 1830s and '40s.[26]

Even more devastating in the lower Columbia and Willamette river valleys was a virulent fever, which is now thought to be malaria. It began in the summer of 1830 and returned each summer for several years afterwards. From a population of somewhat less than 15,600 Chinookan and Kalapuyan people estimated by Lewis and Clark and the Hudson's Bay Company in the early 1800s, the numbers dropped to less than 2,000 by 1841.[27] Cases of the disease in 1831 were reported as far east as the John Day River.[28] The entire population of Sauvie Island appears to have been wiped out by 1833. By that time, the affected area had grown beyond the Willamette Valley to the upper Umpqua, upper Rogue, and perhaps also to Klamath, Modoc, and Paiute tribes in the south central and southeastern parts of the state.[29]

In 1834, the first contingent of Methodist missionaries under Jason Lee arrived in Oregon and set up shop north of Salem at Chemeketa. They expected to find numerous Indian souls to convert but found only two thousand in the entire valley (Kalapuyans, Klikitats, and Molallas).[30] The following year, they created the Willamette Mission School. They claimed to be serving the many children orphaned by the previous years of malaria, but it is likely that children who were not orphans were taken as well. Diseases continued to affect the area, and between 1835 and 1847, the region suffered localized epidemics of meningitis, smallpox, influenza, mumps, and dysentery. The first settlers over the Oregon Trail arrived in 1841, coming across the Columbia Plateau; they brought chicken pox, scarlet fever, and whooping cough to add to the mix. All these sicknesses plagued the population of the school, which was already under great stress, having lost their families and been uprooted from their way of life. One of the more cynical reverends commented that there were "more Indian children in the mission grave-yard ... than there were ... alive in the manual labor school."[31] The school was closed in 1844. That same year four hundred Indians died of dysentery at Fort Vancouver.

In 1847 Indians from the northeast of the state picked up measles on an unsuccessful trip to California to get Spanish cattle and it was subsequently spread to nearly every ethnolinguistic group in the Northwest Coast and Plateau culture areas.[32] Germ theory did not have a strong hold amongst the world populations at that time. Locals saw the diseases as being deliberately aimed at them. It is possible that some disease spreading was done deliberately, but this is hard to prove. We do know, however, that when vaccinations became available, they were given first to Euro-Americans and then to friendly Indians.[33] We also know that some Euro-Americans capitalized on the Indians' beliefs that they had the power to spread sickness. Boyd found evidence of a trader wielding a vial of something, threatening to release the sickness if he didn't get the deal he wanted on furs. Measles ravaged the Cayuse tribe in northeastern Oregon and Washington. Angry Cayuse, suspecting that the missionary Dr. Whitman had something to do with the malady, attacked the mission and killed Dr. Whitman, his wife, and twelve others.

Diseases continued to chip away at the Native population. Measles spread to western Oregon and in July 1848 it was noted in the *Oregon Spectator* that all the lower Umpqua Indians except seven had died of measles and dysentery during the previous winter. An 1878 account states that this epidemic killed half the native population of the Willamette Valley, though a new smallpox epidemic introduced in

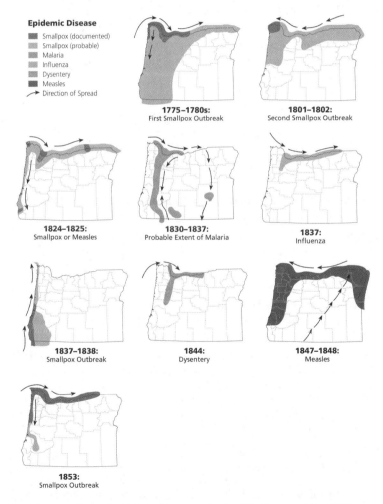

Epidemic Disease
- Smallpox (documented)
- Smallpox (probable)
- Malaria
- Influenza
- Dysentery
- Measles
- Direction of Spread

1775–1780s:
First Smallpox Outbreak

1801–1802:
Second Smallpox Outbreak

1824–1825:
Smallpox or Measles

1830–1837:
Probable Extent of Malaria

1837:
Influenza

1837–1838:
Smallpox Outbreak

1844:
Dysentery

1847–1848:
Measles

1853:
Smallpox Outbreak

Map images from the *Atlas of Oregon* (2nd edition), copyright 2001 University of Oregon Press.

1853 at the mouth of the Columbia, which spread down the coast to Cape Perpetua, certainly must have added to the death toll. What we know is that Lewis and Clark estimated 4,100 natives populating the north Oregon coast in 1805, and only 193 Tillamooks and 155 Alseans were registered in 1854 and 1866 respectively.[34]

When Leo Frachtenburg was doing linguistic research in Western Oregon from 1909 through 1916, diseases were still ravaging the tribes. He wrote to Franz Boas in 1913 and told him that he had planned to leave the Siletz Reservation to interview Kalapuyas on the Grand Ronde Reservation, but he was informed that there were one hundred fifty cases of smallpox at Grand Ronde and every Kalapuya was afflicted. Frachtenburg reported that only two of the thirteen Kalapuya who could still tell stories in their own language were left and one of these was in critical condition.[35]

The Indian populations of the lower Columbia suffered more from introduced diseases than any other subregion of the NW Coast.[36] Boyd has combed through various population assessments through time and estimates that 88 percent of the native population died between approximately 1805 to 1840. Among specific groups the toll was even higher. Ninety-eight percent of the Wappato of Sauvie Island were lost, 92 percent of the Willamette Valley Kalapuya, and 90 percent of the Cascades of the Columbia River. In addition there was an abnormally low percentage of children in the population that was left, making population renewal all the more difficult.[37] The numerous overloaded Indian cemeteries that were commented on by early Euro-American arrivals were looted and scattered and no longer stand as a testament to the era of decimation by introduced diseases.[38]

The impact of disease found its way into the oral literature of the area. The Sun's Myth collected from the Chinook informant Charles Cultee by Franz Boas in 1891 evokes the feeling that must have prevailed during times of epidemics. It shows an incipient understanding of the vector of human-borne disease.

> *all his town he would destroy*
> *and he would destroy his relatives.*
> *He would recover:*
> *his town (is) nothing*
> *the dead fill the ground.*[39]

The disappearance of entire villages is also referenced in the myth "Coyote, Turkey, Buzzard, and the Disease," collected by Melville Jacobs in 1928 from John Hudson, one of the last speakers of Santiam

Kalapuya. In this story Coyote says, "Where do you come from? Have they not all died where you have come from?"[40]

Knowing about this decimation is crucial to understanding the history of Oregon native languages. The most important safeguard against language death is obviously having many speakers. The population of several Oregon language groups dropped so low at this time that maintenance of certain languages became problematic.

Reservations

Treaty making began in the 1850s, though southern Oregon was still in turmoil. That area was a major thoroughfare to the California gold mines and gold was discovered in Jacksonville, Oregon, in 1851. Many Euro-Americans settled in the area on their donation claims with large herds of sheep and cattle. Mining and ranching competed with hunting and gathering and the two groups got off to a bad start, descending into a cycle of violence. In 1852, Ben Wright (who was married to an Indian woman) orchestrated the murder of forty-two Modocs in one night. In 1854 sixteen Indians were murdered during the night at the mouth of the Coquille River.[41] By 1855, four treaties had been made and four Indian Agencies set up: Umatilla, Warm Springs, Grand Ronde, and Coast (later called Siletz). The Klamath Reservation was not established until 1864 and the Malheur Reservation until 1872. By that year, according to a report by Francis Walker, Commissioner of Indian Affairs, there were 9,633 Indians on Oregon reservations and another three thousand or so who had no treaty relations with the government and were not under the charge of any agent.[42] It was also in that year that some of the Modocs from the Klamath Reservation left and began fighting with the Euro-Americans for their own reservation at Lost River. Instead, after being defeated, the leaders were hung and the rest of the band was sent to Oklahoma.

Oregon had its own versions of the "Trail of Tears," as people were herded up like animals and forced by soldiers to walk to reservations far from their homes. One of these forced marches involved Indians from southern Oregon and northern California who were made to walk to the newly established Coast Reservation.[43] One Siletz tribal member told her grandmother's story of the march:

> Some families were even broken up, maybe a mother in one
> bunch and her children in another bunch. Many fled to the
> mountains, for they did not want to leave their homes. But
> they learned quickly that if they wanted to live they dared not

*protest. ... She told of women being abused, misused, and
even kicked by the white soldiers, especially if a mother tried
to protect her young daughters. If men came to the rescue of
their families, they were badly beaten and in some cases shot
and left, for they were not allowed to stop and bury anyone
along the way. She also remembered little children being
kicked around if they fell too far behind. ... When they got to
Siletz, she told of how hungry, how tired and weary and, yes,
how heartsick, for there they were on the most rugged part of
the coast. Lands were not cleared. The climate was different;
it was like going to a foreign country. She remembered a lot
of people dying from many different diseases unknown to her,
probably chicken pox, tuberculosis, she did not know. For she
always believed most of them died of depression, heartbreak,
and mistreatment.*[44]

Hall reported that many of the Coquille believed that the forced
marches and boat trips, followed by years spent in forts and on
temporary reservations under difficult living conditions and in
obligatory contact with Euro-Americans and Indians with different
languages and cultures, led to the obliteration of much of their
ancestors' cultural knowledge. The multilingualism of the reservations
was different in kind from the multilingualism that preceded Euro-
American settlement. In the earlier multilingualism, people had
a choice of which languages to learn, or in other words, who to
associate with. The reservations presented a forced multilingualism
among people who had been, in some way, "defeated." Often former
enemies found themselves living right next to one another with no
power to change the situation. We know that the U.S. government
recognized the multilingualism of the reservations because one of the
standard operating expenses of the various Indian agencies was the
salary for interpreters and these were never for one single language.
For instance, two interpreters were on the payroll at Klamath Agency.
In 1868, C. Preston translated for both Klamath and Modoc, which
are closely related, though their speakers were not always on friendly
terms. The other translator, J. Hood, was for the Snake Indians.[45]
Women commonly served as translators: Chetco Jennie, Sarah
Winnemucca, and the Modoc woman, Winema, were all well-known
translators. Women were often brought in from other tribes through
purchase or kidnapping, so the necessity of learning another language
often fell on the shoulders of women.

The Indian Council at Walla Walla in May and June 1855 as described by Colonel Lawrence Kip contains some interesting insights into the language practices of the Plateau tribes, indicating the verbal skills of this highly oral culture. Governor Stevens had summoned the tribes in order to purchase their land and remove them to reservations. (He succeeded in getting them to cede thirty-one million acres in what is now southeastern Washington and northeastern Oregon.) About five thousand Native Americans were there, representing about eight tribes. The Nez Perce delivered their speeches and sermons line by line. One chief would say a line and another repeated that line in a louder voice, ensuring that the message was heard and understood. The Cayuse were observed improvising songs on a variety of topics. English speeches were translated sentence by sentence into both Nez Perce and Walla Walla. One of the translators was a Delaware Indian from the East Coast. By this time several Nez Perce had adopted Christianity and had learned to read and write. Kip mentions that two or three Nez Perce who could write were keeping a minute account of all that transpired at the meetings. How wonderful to be able to access those transcripts and compare them to the accounts of the Euro-Americans in attendance—but although the staff at Tamástslikt Archives has been searching for years, they still have not found the Nez Perce accounts and fear they have been lost forever. In the absence of written native accounts, we need to pay closer attention to oral traditions and to the multivocality of texts written by Euro-Americans. This has been called "reading against the grain," finding in gaps and random insertions clues to how others might have experienced the event. (The way Native Americans can use materials written by Euro-Americans in revitalizing languages and cultures will be described in more detail in chapter four.)

Colonel Kip's account is a multivocal. It lacks the monological cast of official government reports in which it is assumed that the path taken by the U.S. government officials is correct and moral. In Kip's report, for instance, he recounts a touching speech by a Cayuse chief. The chief asked,

> I wonder if the ground has anything to say? I wonder if the ground is listening to what is said? I wonder if the ground would come alive and what is on it? Though I hear what the ground says. The ground says, "It is the Great Spirit that placed me here. The Great Spirit tells me to take care of the Indians, to feed them aright. The Great Spirit appointed the roots to feed the Indians on." The water says the same thing.

"The Great Spirit directs me. Feed the Indians well." The grass says the same thing. "Feed the horses and cattle." The ground, water, and grass say, "The Great Spirit has given us our names. We have these names and hold these names. Neither the Indians or whites have a right to change these names."[46]

We do not know whether this was the chief's own translation into English or someone else's, but even through the cracks in translation that we might find, the chief's words indicate a very different way of looking at the environment and language. He invites the earth, the rivers, and the plants into the treaty negotiation. For him, these are animate beings who should have a say. The way in which the natural environment attains animacy through language is very different from the capitalist worldview within which land became a mere commodity. Another interesting clue to a different language ideology in this short passage is the statement that the Great Spirit gave them their names and no one had a right to change these names. We could see this as a belief in a natural or nonarbitrary link between the thing and its name, but since these people were well aware of multilingualism (which belies a natural link between sound and meaning), we might look to a more metaphorical meaning. By "changing the names" could the chief have meant "changing the purpose to which they are put"? This interpretation fits with the pervasive theme of "feeding the Indians" in the passage. There was an understanding that the land would no longer be used for feeding the Indians through hunting and foraging, but for feeding the whites through agriculture. We often find that places are named according to their use. In this case, changing the use would, indeed, change the name.

The reservation system compromised native ways of life and dealt another blow to the maintenance of Oregon languages. Indians were herded onto reservations and subsistence activities based on free access to the land and its resources were highly curtailed. John Hudson dictated the following prophecy between 1928 and 1936 in the Santiam dialect of Kalapuya:

In the old time, by the forks of the Santiam
a Kalapuya man lay down in an alder-grove
and dreamed his farthest dream. When he woke in the night
he told the people, "This earth beneath us
was all black, all black in my dream!"
No man could say what it meant,
that dream of our greening earth.

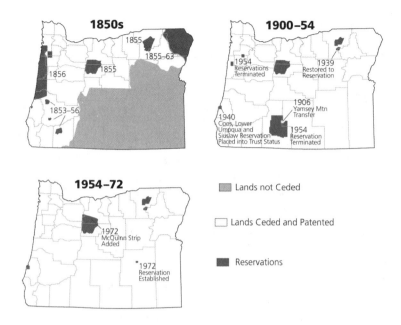

Map images from the *Atlas of Oregon* (2nd edition), copyright 2001
University of Oregon Press.

> *We forgot. But then the white men came,*
> *those iron farmers, and we saw them plow up the ground,*
> *the camas meadow, the little prairies by the Santiam,*
> *and we knew we would enter their dream*
> *of the earth plowed black forever.*[47]

Not only were Native Oregonians confined to reservations, but
these reservation lands continually shrank through time, as you
can see in the maps above. As Euro-American settlers discovered
desirable land on the reservations, their borders were readjusted.
Under the allotment policy in the late 1880s, collectively owned
tribal lands were converted to private ownership. These plots were
frequently sold to non-Indians, creating a patchwork of ownership
within reservation borders. The sizeable Malheur Reservation was
simply dissolved in retaliation for the participation of a few bands of
Paiute in the 1878 Bannock War. In the 1950s entire tribes were told
that they no longer constituted a Native American group and their
reservations were legally terminated along with their identity. The
Klamath Tribes lost a reservation of 1.8 million acres when they were
terminated from federal recognition.

New technology and ways of living were taught in English and traditional ways of living were talked about in Indian languages. As the new rhythm of life took over, traditional ways of living and the languages associated with them lost status. People speaking several languages were forced together on reservations: Sahaptin tribes, Northern Paiute, and Wasco on the Warm Springs Reservation; Umatilla, Nez Perce, Walla Walla, Palouse, and Cayuse on the Umatilla Reservation; Klamath, Modoc, and Northern Paiute on the Klamath Reservation. Along the coast, linguistic conditions were even more diverse. On the Grand Ronde and Siletz reservations, where remnants of the western tribes were grouped, people spoke over twenty-five different dialects from probably a half dozen language families, originally spoken from southern Washington to northern California. When Indian agents went to these areas, they often brought people who could translate into multiple languages. No doubt, subsequent translations were done for people who spoke one of the lesser-used languages in the earlier years of reservation life and there was always Chinuk Wawa, but over time English became the new lingua franca of Oregon reservations. Of course, language shift is never smooth and some families maintained a Native language in the home well into the twentieth century. By this time, though, all but the elders also spoke English.

Reservations and Federally Recognized Tribes

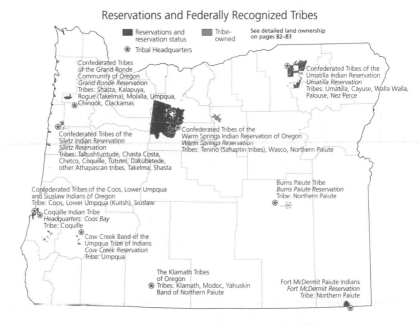

Boarding Schools

When Native people are asked the reason their language is no longer spoken, the most common response is "boarding schools." The purpose of boarding schools was to make Indian children follow Euro-American ways of life. This involved new ways of looking at the land as something to be owned and tilled. Native languages were targeted for destruction along with native ways of life that did not fit the vision of nineteenth-century American nationalists.

The first school in Oregon for the mixed-race children of fur traders was at Fort Vancouver. This was followed by schools set up by missionaries. The Methodist Mission School that ran from 1835 to 1844 was mentioned earlier. It was plagued by sickness. The first year there were fourteen Indian students, of whom seven died and five ran away. The Catholic mission school for boys opened in 1843 in St. Paul and the one for girls opened the following year. The Presbyterians set up missions with schools just across the present-day Oregon borders in Washington and Idaho. Missionaries attempted to learn the native languages because it was easier to convert people if you had a command of their language.

Native languages were tolerated at first in the Catholic mission school set up in St. Paul in western Oregon. By 1839, Father Demers, who was known for his linguistic abilities, had translated several religious texts into Chinook Jargon. His vocabulary lists were required studying for the nuns who voyaged from Belgium around the tip of South America to arrive at the Columbia River in 1844. These European women were brought in to instruct the children of the community of St. Paul in the Willamette Valley. In addition to the children, several of the elderly Indian women and younger "half-breed" women joined their classes in the field. Everyone understood Chinook Jargon and the Vicar General assisted the nuns in teaching the women prayers in Chinook Jargon. After they had mastered a few, he repeated them over and over in French, hoping that his pupils would "come to sense a spiritual meaning which Chinook could never convey."[48] Even before the nuns arrived, they were told that the French element in Chinook Jargon was growing since the "young half-breeds tended to add French expressions to the Chinook of their mothers."[49] However, by the following year, Father Demers had changed his mind about how important it was for the nuns to learn Chinook Jargon and for the Indians to learn French. The American population was growing and he was receiving multiple requests for classes conducted in English. He was disappointed in the small amount of English that the nuns had mastered and predicted that the Indians would pick up English and forget Chinook.[50] The diary entries of the Belgian nuns allude to a very dynamic linguistic situation in the Willamette Valley. Chinook Jargon was incorporating more French expressions and English was beginning to push out French as the language of prestige.

Mission schools were abandoned by the 1850s as federally run day schools were established. Christian missionaries, however, remained in charge of many of these schools. Many treaties called for the establishment of schools, and by the 1860s, there were schools in Siletz, Grand Ronde, Rogue River, Umpqua, Willamette Valley, Warm Springs, and Umatilla. Later, schools were established in Klamath and Yainax. Already, language had become an issue, illustrated in this 1868 Report of Indian Peace Commissioners: "In the difference of language today lies two-thirds of our trouble … Schools should be established, which children should be required to attend; their barbarous dialect should be blotted out and the English language substituted."[51] In 1870 Congress appropriated $100,000 for the establishment of federal industrial schools for Indians. First they funded day schools on the reservations. In 1872 the Umatilla school had twenty-seven pupils; the Warm Springs school had fifty-one; the Grand Ronde School had fifty; and the Siletz school had twenty.[52]

Many early European educators wrote about the children's quickness and desire to learn. They also mentioned a high rate of absenteeism at times of the year when traditional food-gathering events took place. They noticed that while the children were in school, they practiced European ways, but once they left, they went back to Indian ways. Rather than seeing the ability to act appropriately in two cultures as desirable, many educators took this as evidence that the format of the education system was failing.

Federal agents concluded that, in order to make Americans out of these Indian children, their native languages and cultures must be destroyed. The best way to do this was to break the natural transmission between elders and youngsters. Day schools fell out of favor and more effort was put into boarding schools, where children could be separated from Native American culture.

A letter from the Indian Agent at Siletz in 1859 clearly states this desire:

> *If the government would establish a separate reservation for all of the children over 3 and under ten years of age, and never allow the older Indians to visit them, we could then civilize the rising generation. The children could be taught*

> *to repeat the English language, and forgetting their horrible*
> *superstitions, they would then be prepared to receive a*
> *Christian education.*[53]

The first Indian boarding schools were located right on the reservations. Children could look out and see their homes, but were not allowed to leave the school. State agents kidnapped children and placed them in boarding schools, where they were punished for speaking their native languages. It was so common for Indian children to run away from school that there was a specific question on this topic on the monthly school reports that had to be submitted. For example, we can see that during October 1882 at the Siletz Indian Day school, six children were withdrawn or ran away.[54]

Examining the curriculum of these schools, it is clear that the intent was not to create equal citizens out of the Indians, but to train them to do domestic work and manual labor and to be able to understand English. A letter written by the teacher at the Grand Ronde school back to the Commissioner for Indian Affairs on September 12th, 1887, described a situation in which schoolwork was given last priority and the free labor of the "students" was exploited as they were forced to do manual work all day long and at night their clothes froze in the ill-equipped dormitories.[55] Their parents complained bitterly. Some even insisted that their children should get paid for their work. An 1887 report praising the school at Yainax claimed that "the girls are farther advanced in their ability for housework, cooking, and kitchen management than any other Indian girls I have seen." Later the author of the report, J. B. Harrison, called them "more capable, intelligent, and faithfully efficient in their work than the average of servants in New England towns."[56] He did not think that any good would come of trying to make Indian scholars. He wrote that they would "be disadvantaged in competition with white men."[57] Given the blatant discrimination of the time, this was certainly true, but to decide not to prepare children for roles, anticipating unfair treatment, presents a case of pre-emptive discrimination that leaves no room for societal change.

Harrison did, however, join other commentators of his time in railing against incompetent teachers in the Indian schools. It is true that their duties extended far beyond teaching classroom subjects. They were in charge of room and board and "industrial" training and they often did not receive the supplies they expected. Perhaps most importantly, they did not understand the cultures in which they were placed. Unable to surmount the cultural differences, some teachers simply shut the schools down. When the new superintendent at Siletz, John McCain, wrote to the commissioner of Indian Affairs on April 12th, 1889, he told him that the school had not been in session from the 30th of last June until the 18th of March.[58] It is hard to maintain consistency with this sort of schedule.

Incompetence was not as serious as predatory behavior. Indian Agent B. R. Biddle wrote to William Dole, Commissioner of Indian Affairs on June 30th, 1862, explaining that nothing at Siletz deserved to be called a school. People who were hired "conducted themselves in such an immoral manner as to inspire the Indians with contempt … the Indians have been led to believe that the whites were only here to gratify their lusts, rather than for any good purpose."[59] Parents at the Siletz Agency school grew reluctant to send their children there, especially their older girls.

1887 was a fateful year for American Indians. The Dawes Act turned reservation land held in common into individual ownership, and federal law forbade Native American languages in the classroom. The United States at that time was setting up an ideological agenda in opposition to the growing interest in socialism in Europe. American Indian ways of life were seen as socialistic and had to be replaced with values of individualism and private initiative. What better way to erase their previous life than to erase the very language that they learned it through.

A letter from the Siletz Indian Agent, J. B. Lane, to the Commissioner of Indian Affairs on July 26th, 1887, estimated the price of gathering up Indian children living along the coast to be $300. The reasons given for the high price included: "[T]he coast line is very much broken and the Indians scattered for a long distance and the parents are much averse to giving up their children."[60] Forcing parents to "give up" their children tore apart Indian families and left children in cold institutions bereft of parenting models. Usually, the first thing that was done to the boys was to cut their hair. This was an act of mourning in many tribes and, in retrospect, seems very fitting, metaphorically, though the significance bypassed the perpetrators of the act.

Chemawa Indian school (established first in Forest Grove in 1890 and then in Salem, where it remains today) was the second remote federal boarding school established in Oregon and is the oldest one still running. It followed the dominant approach of the time, including 1) removal from home and tribal influences; 2) strict military discipline, including short haircuts and uniforms; and 3) teaching of the Protestant work ethic.[61] Native methods and subjects were broached in the area of art only. At first, Chemawa drew largely from tribes in Oregon and neighboring states. It appears that there was some pressure put on Indian agents to send students from their schools to the Forest Grove campus.[62] By 1924, the school comprised seventy buildings on 450 acres serving students from all around the Northwest and Alaska. It was largely self-supporting with students learning and practicing animal husbandry and farming, as well as the basics of reading and writing in English. One report on Chemawa stated:

> *The first rule here after cleanliness and obedience is "No Indian Talk." The delegations from different tribes are divided and subdivided until all tribal association is broken up and lost. Over and over again and all the time are the children impressed with the fact that if they only learn to speak English well their coming is a grand success for them and their people. This and their entire removal from family and reservation influences are the points of highest hope.[63]*

In 1930 there were 1,171 Oregon Indian children in schools.[64] At that time there was only one reservation boarding school left. It was on the Warm Springs Reservation and could hold 113 students from the first through sixth grades.[65] Chemawa in Salem was one of nineteen non-reservation boarding schools nationally. It had a capacity of 750 students from grades four through twelve. By this time, the majority of its student population came from tribes outside the state. In fact, while no Oregon Native language has ever been taught at Chemawa, there were several years beginning in 1948 during which the entire curriculum was available in Navajo, and one fifth of the students were non-English-speaking Navajos.[66]

Almost fifty years after J. B. Lane wrote about snatching children from their parents, the process continued. Testimony by Dana Coolidge before the Senate subcommittee of the Committee on Indian Affairs in 1932 included:

> *I am making a brief statement of my experience with what I consider the greatest shame of the Indian Service—the rounding up of Indian children to be sent away to government boarding schools. The business of "kid catching," as it is called, is rarely discussed with outsiders, either by the Indians or by the government employees.[67]*

One of the teachers of Oregon languages today, Gilbert Towner, was kidnapped under this despicable practice. He told of his experience as a five-year-old in southwestern Oregon about 1933:

*Well, I lived in an area that everybody knew, was an area
where no English was spoken. And the government went to
these areas and gathered up all of the kids, and sent us off to
Chemawa. And I never had the consent of my parents or my
grandmother. They just gathered us up and took us over there,
to, what they called, Americanize us, and to rid us of speaking
our language.*

Since Indians had been deemed "wards of the government,"
Gilbert's parents and grandparents could not protest his being taken
away. He described what life was like at the Indian boarding school:

*There were five of us boys from that area in one room,
and when we were brought into the classroom, we didn't
understand what they were saying, because they were talking
in English, and they would whip us for speaking our language,
and by whipping, I mean with a leather strap. I didn't know
why I was being whipped, and I tried to run away. I didn't
know where home was, but I was running away, and trying to
get home. They'd catch me every time, take me back, and whip
me for running away. So those years were pretty hard.*

At the most fundamental level, language maintenance depends on
attitudes toward that language. The denigration of native languages
in Indian boarding schools transmitted the idea that these languages,
which had long carried the culture of the indigenous people of Oregon,
were not worth speaking to one's children. At the same time, cultures
and languages prove incredibly resistant when people take pride in
them. Let's return to Gilbert Towner's report of life at Chemawa.

*One time, a bunch of us boys went down to Pigville [where
they kept the pigs in Chemawa] and somebody brought
down an old washtub, and some of the guys cut feathers out
of cardboard, and they tied little cans around our legs, and
we had our own pow-wow going. And they caught us, and I
thought we were going to get whipped bad again, but they took
us in the gymnasium, and they called all of the students there,
and all of the teachers and the staff, instructors, and they
told us to go out in the middle of the floor, and do the same
things we did down there at Pigville, and so we did. We started
dancing, and pretty soon, one by one, the kids started coming
off the benches, and joined in, and even the Indian teachers,
they come out, and so it sort of defeated their humiliation. ...*

They were trying to make an example out of us. But everybody joined in, so it defeated them. ... It was pretty good.

I've always been struck by the cinematic potential of this story. The boys had been wrenched from their families and cultures and kept as virtual prisoners in a boarding school in order to make them into Christian farmers. Their own dances and clothing were mocked. Sent down to care for the pigs, they used the refuse of the new society to fashion replicas of traditional regalia and remember the dances they practiced before being separated from their culture. When the authorities discovered them, I can just hear them talking amongst themselves about how ridiculous the boys looked and what better way to denigrate these practices than to make a spectacle of them in front of the whole school. Let the errant boys suffer the ridicule of the school community. The tension builds as the whole school is assembled. Were the boys scared and reluctant to perform in front of the crowd, or did the words of their elders telling them, "[B]e proud of who you are," ring in their ears? Probably both emotions were present. I can see the camera focus in on their faces as they begin to dance, hesitatingly at first. Then, with more energy, as they see the Indian teachers in the audience stand and begin dancing towards them. The camera pans to the audience and we see the children slipping down from the bleachers to join them as the non-Indian staff is left looking at each other in bewilderment.

At the same time that I see this scene so clearly in my head, I also wonder whether the response of the school authorities to create an assembly around the children's dancing was the result of implementing Collier's reforms in Bureau of Indian Affairs schools. John Collier, the new Commissioner of Indian Affairs in 1933, had great appreciation for Native American cultures and was very much against the alienating effects of Indian boarding schools. He had several of them closed during his tenure and Chemawa was threatened with closure. Collier's reforms had a profound effect on the academic achievement of Indian students. In 1928, 6 percent of Indian students were performing academically at the age-appropriate grade level, and by 1946, the figure was 36 percent. So, an alternate interpretation would have the Chemawa staff looking for evidence of Native culture that they could showcase in their school to demonstrate to their higher-ups that Chemawa respected Indian cultures. If this interpretation might be closer to the truth as seen by the authorities, it clearly only confused the children. The ideological shift that redefined their dancing from "transgression" to "valued cultural practice" was not apparent to children who had become accustomed to authoritarian rulers who did not change their minds.

Conclusion

Native Americans speaking a variety of different languages and sustaining themselves in the vastly different ecosystems of this state came under attack by invisible germs before they came to know the more conscious forms of attack. Not only did the invaders bring diseases to which the Natives had no natural immunities, but they also brought advanced weaponry that early settlers used against Native Americans with impunity. In addition, Native American cultures and the languages that embodied them were assaulted. Often the perpetrators of these cultural and linguistic assaults were well-meaning Euro-Americans who thought that it was in the best interest of Native Americans to be more like them: Christian agriculturalists who spoke English. With this philosophy, they set out to obliterate Native American languages. Confining Native Americans speaking multiple languages on ever-shrinking reservations and separating children from parents and grandparents in boarding schools were two of the principal weapons in this attack.

One might think, given the population decimation, land privation, and harsh education policies, in conjunction with the general lack of knowledge about Native languages in Oregon, that these languages would have disappeared entirely. Yet this is not the case. We would be the last to claim that there are thriving speech communities using Native languages in the state, but the amazing thing is that Native languages have survived at all. The following chapter addresses the ways in which Native languages of Oregon have persisted.

Chapter Two

Resistance to Monolingualism: Reviving our Languages

Joan Gross

Introduction

When the first Europeans arrived in Oregon, it appears that the most common Native response was curiosity and an interest in the new trade goods that the Europeans brought with them. As the numbers of newcomers increased, however, and they began imposing their way of life on the people and natural environment of the state, Native Americans began to resist the encroachment. They resisted by not allowing themselves to be completely assimilated into the new culture and by practicing their own ways of life and speaking their own languages.

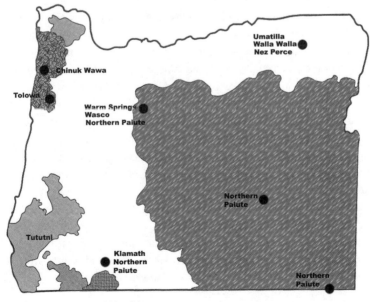

Language Revitalization Projects

Map by Loretta Wardrip

This chapter focuses on Native Americans in Oregon who are involved in the revitalization of their languages as teachers and learners. Today there are efforts to revitalize ten of these languages (Cayuse-Nez Perce, Chinuk Wawa, Klamath, Northern Paiute, Tolowa, Tututni, Umatilla, Walla Walla, Warm Springs, and Wasco).[1] Some language programs have been established for several years and others are just beginning. Three of the language programs encompass several of the languages spoken on the reservation. The Confederated Tribes of Warm Springs teach Warm Springs Wasco and Northern Paiute. The language program of the Confederated Tribes of the Umatilla encompasses Cayuse-Nez Perce, Umatilla, and Walla Walla. The Klamath Tribes have recently begun supporting a Northern Paiute teacher in addition to their work on Klamath. This complicates their mission at the same time that it respects the multilingual pattern of traditional Native American life in this area. There are also individuals who have put a lot of work into learning a language of their ancestors without the benefit of a language program. Our focus here is on individuals within programs that have some level of institutional support. Though the level of support from tribal councils and from public schools varies greatly from one program to the next and funding fluctuates from year to year, all the programs have teachers who struggle with curriculum and at least a few students who are eager to learn.

During 2004 and 2005, we interviewed fifty-two Oregon Natives who are administrators of tribal language programs, Native language teachers, and students. Similar themes emerged from these interviews that I will address in this chapter. First, I examine the generational linkages through which indigenous languages were maintained in some families, then the way people temporarily "lost" their language. Most teachers of Oregon languages today did not continuously speak their native language. Some of them spoke the language when they were young and then went through a period of several years when they didn't speak it. Others didn't speak it or spoke very little when they were young, but put great effort into learning it as young adults. Both groups went through a process of "discovering" their ancestral language. The first group went through a process of remembering the language while the second had to learn it anew. The final part of the chapter focuses on their experiences of breathing new life into Oregon Native languages. I hope that reading the words of Native Oregonians will give the reader an enriched understanding of what it means to be an indigenous person with a heritage language.

Resisting Assimilation

Native American resistance has taken different forms over the years. Violent resistance (pictured in numerous cinematic battles between "cowboys" and Indians) became the center-piece of American Western stories. To be a "good guy" was to be a Euro-American cowboy, so that's what many Indian kids chose when they were role-playing these battles. In real life, when Indians massacred Euro-Americans, the incident was publicized widely and much effort went into finding the perpetrators and hanging them, as was the case in what was called "the Whitman Massacre." When Euro-Americans massacred Native Americans (a much more common scenario) it seldom received much publicity. Alternative stories continued through oral traditions in Indian families. Malissa Minthorn of Tamástslikt Cultural Institute discussed this in her interview:

> Oftentimes we know what we know because our parents taught us. Everybody learns about the Oregon Trail in the fourth grade, and that we were mass murderers and savages and we did these horrible things. Of course, from our own perspectives, we would say, "[B]ut that is not what our people say," and we were basically chopped off at the knees and were told, "That is not true. This is the truth because it's in print, and this is what we are teaching." So there is a lot of frustration and anger that our own cultural knowledge has not been accurately reflected in the written record.

The telling of alternative versions of historical events in the family represents another type of resistance to Euro-American assimilation. We can call this "positive resistance," since it reinforces Native culture in the face of newly imposed societal norms. This type of resistance has been far more important to language retention and revitalization than violent resistance. Families that practiced positive cultural resistance often were cognizant of needing a certain separation from the dominant culture. To accomplish this they hid their children from government agents sent to take them to boarding school. They avoided the fast-growing towns and cities and often moved farther out into forests and deserts. In these more isolated settings, it was easier for them to continue to speak Native languages in the home and pass them down naturally to their children.

A Wasco elder told us how her own grandmother was hidden from the Bureau of Indian Affairs agents by her grandmother and so never learned English.

> *Well, some of our people, they didn't go to school, so they*
> *talked just their own language. My grandmother was one of*
> *them; she didn't go to school. Her sisters and brothers did.*
> *They were put in school, but she, her grandmother hid her.*
> [laughing] *She didn't let her go. So she didn't learn English.*

Children had their own ways of resisting U.S. educational policy focused on cutting ties between Indian children and their elders; they simply ran away every chance they could get. Reports by early school directors constantly bemoan the high absentee rate. Other children withdrew within themselves, passively resisting Euro-American education. This strategy puts psychological, rather than physical, distance between the home and the dominant assimilationist culture.

Psychological distance was also achieved through the sacred realm, where Indians could separate themselves from the dominant culture and surround themselves with prayers and songs in their native languages.[2] To this day, the religious domain is where Native languages have remained strongest and this imparts a sacredness to the languages in general. Mildred Quaempts, speaker/teacher of Umatilla, has tried to reconstruct immersion situations, but finds that the best place for her students to see the relevance of the language is at longhouse ceremonies.

> *Well, I guess the best space is the longhouse, we speak a lot of*
> *the language there. We want our children to learn as much as*
> *they can. The language comes up in the ceremonies, so they'll*
> *know when we say commands like "sit down" and "stand up,"*
> *"raise your hand, turn around, drink your water" ... Be able*
> *to know all that. We've had students that have said "After I*
> *took the class, I was able to sit there and listen and I could*
> *understand some of the words comin' out."*

The language helped people resist assimilation because it connected them to their culture. It provided access to a worldview that differed from the dominant Euro-American one that was promoted in the schools and other institutions.

Linking the Generations

Myra Johnson, director of the language program of the Confederated Tribes of Warm Springs, perceptively spoke of the well-known colonial method of divide and conquer. We are used to this concept being used to refer to splitting up tribes and forcing them to live apart in distant reservations, but Johnson used the term to refer to the damage that was done to Indian families. Children were separated from their parents and grandparents, breaking the most important of human ties. We saw how this was blatantly done through boarding schools, but more subtle characteristics of culture change were imposed later. For instance, public housing projects constructed houses for nuclear families, ignoring traditional living patterns that involved extended families and multiple-family groups. Gone were the longhouses where several generations of several families lived together. Children became more isolated from their older relatives.

Languages link different groups of people together. In situations of language shift, older and younger generations often lose the means with which to communicate. Just as learning a language creates a connection with other speakers of that language, retaining a family language creates connections with older generations. Intergenerational living patterns were diametrically opposed to the United States boarding school policy that specifically broke the links between generations of Indian families. Multiple-generational living did exactly the reverse, reinforcing links between the generations.

Fluent speakers of Oregon Native languages today almost exclusively grew up with their grandparents as primary caregivers. For the most part, people talk about their grandmothers as dominant Native language speakers who couldn't or wouldn't speak English. They all expressed a deep interest in and respect for the ways of their grandparents. This interest set them apart from the majority of kids their age. Fred Hill, teacher of Umatilla, had this to say:

> *I do feel fortunate. I don't boast about having learned the language, I just feel fortunate that I was raised by my grandmother. Sometimes I wish I coulda knew my mother and my father but that wasn't the case so having learned the languages through my grandmother and my uncle and all the rest of 'em, some of the elders. I used to get ridiculed because I used to hang around the elders. "Why don't you hang around us, we're doin' all this stuff? How come you hang around them? You always do things 'old fashioned.'"*

The continued practice of one's language is one facet of positive resistance. This became increasingly difficult as confederated tribes strove to make their voices heard in American political circles. The dominance of English, backed by the strongest media industry in the world, slowly began making its way into Native American homes. We must recognize, too, that the new system was very patriarchal and the traditional roles played by older women were neither understood nor valued. This marginalized segment of the population became keepers of traditional ways, including language. Gilbert Towner, teacher of Tututni, who is in his seventies, had this to say about his grandmother:

> *[My grandmother] lived practically the old ways. I would catch a lot of salmon and take them to her, and she would cut them up and wind-dry them, and I would take a lot of that salmon to the old people, and that's how she taught me to take care of the old people, and hunt for them, and maybe just go to their house and carry water for them, or cut wood for them. And that's what I did; I wasn't like a lot of other young people who would like to do whatever was popular during the time, and I became pretty serious about what I was doing, and not really smart in the things of the day. But then she always told me to be proud of who I was, to always hold your head up, because there was nothing to be ashamed of. If you spoke your language, that was nothing to be ashamed of.*

Willy Sigo is only in his twenties, and is studying Umatilla now, but his early memories were of his great-grandmother speaking to him in Nez Perce.

> *I'd always go over to my great-grandmother's house and I'd just sit down in her lap and she'd just talk with me or we'd go to the table and we couldn't leave the table until we were all fully done with our food and we'd have to ask for it in Indian. And so I always knew that there was our language and the English language.*

A couple of the language teachers today grew up with grandparents who insisted that English not be spoken around them. At the same time, it is interesting to note that all these elders knew more than one indigenous language. This speaks to a shift in linguistic ideology from a multilingual indigenous perspective to a monolingual American English one in later generations. People who speak multiple languages enjoy the possibilities multilingualism provides and they don't fear the far too common attitude that learning a second language will somehow diminish one's abilities in the first. They relish the opportunities multilingualism gives them both for communicating with different people and for masking their communication from others. They also appreciate the way that reflecting on languages brings out interesting similarities and differences in the way people express themselves. This gives them great insight into the influence of language on worldview. Umatilla elder Inez Reeves exemplifies the multilingual past. When I asked her about her uncle and her dad speaking Chinuk Wawa, she answered:

> *They were always trying to teach somebody different words,*
> *but I didn't care to listen to that 'cause I was more interested*
> *in our own languages because I can speak Nez Perce and*
> *Umatilla and I can understand the Yakima and Warm Springs*
> *and the River People down here at Celilo.*

The local linguist Noel Rude agreed, adding that Reeves was also a good Walla Walla informant. The late Neva Eggsman, who was the pillar of the Klamath language program, spoke Modoc as well as Klamath and English. Several of our younger interviewees spoke of their older relatives speaking multiple native languages. Manny Calapoo said that both his great-grandmother and grandmother spoke Shoshone, Paiute, Wasco, and Warm Springs. Sigo said, "My grandma's still alive. I think she said she speaks Umatilla, Walla Walla, and some Wasco, some Warm Springs." Jess Nowland's great-great-grandma's husband was Charlie Celilo. He got his name from spending so much time at Celilo Falls, the central fishing and trading area of the Columbia River before the dam went in. Nowland said that Charlie could speak eight Indian languages, the languages of all the tribes who came there. Clearly these people have placed a lot of importance on the ability to communicate with others.

Respect for one's elders has been key to maintaining Native cultural practices and thus can be seen as a major form of positive resistance in Indian communities. By elevating the experience of elders, Native Americans showed that they valued cultural practices that had lost prestige in the new mainstream society. Maintaining a Native worldview (too narrowly defined as religion) meant respecting animals and plants as relatives, a view that is diametrically opposed to the extractive mentality brought by early Europeans who were primarily interested in converting natural resources into cash.

An elder is not simply an old person. An elder is someone who is willing to share the wisdom of their past for the good of their people. Myra Johnson put it this way:

> *Elders see all things and offer you a good feeling when you*
> *are down, have good things to say to you or good things to*

share, or they share the wisdom of their past, I guess. Those,
to me, are the elders. Those that really have a heart for the
people.

Most elders today have not spoken their language continuously, but
have disconnected and reconnected with their language at different
times in their lives. They are at a point in their lives when they realize
the importance of some of the things that they undervalued when
younger. Karen Crutcher realized this when she discovered that her
own father, who wouldn't teach her Paiute as a child, was teaching it
to her son whenever he went for a visit.

Losing a Language

It is typical for people not to recognize that their language is losing
ground until it is almost too late to reverse the decline. Language
shift often happens as unconsciously as language acquisition. It is
an uneven process and occurs in some families earlier than in others.
Janice George-Hill's family maintained Sahaptin in the home long
after most families had shifted to English. Throughout the 1960s,
however, they assumed that everyone else was speaking Sahaptin
in the home too. Then, George-Hill began to realize that her own
cousins were already speaking mostly in English. Her immediate
family felt compelled to shift to English after she was rejected from
kindergarten.

> *As a child I grew up in the language ... I was the only child*
> *among a household of adults and so they were always*
> *speaking, so I was always in that, in it daily. So when I started*
> *school, they didn't have the Head Start or day care like they*
> *do now, so I didn't attend preschool. So when I started first*
> *grade I was there for about, I think less than a week, and it*
> *was really hard for me to pick up on the English and so the*
> *principal called up my parents and said, "We can't, she needs*
> *to come back next year." They needed for them to talk to me in*
> *English so I could pick up the English. The Indian language*
> *was our primary language and so I didn't come back until the*
> *following year. My parents just had to talk to me in English.*

George-Hill's parents were supportive of her getting an education,
so they began speaking to her in English and she entered school
the following year. She found that as she got more educated, she
stopped using her native language except when they would go to the
Longhouse. She noticed a clear shift to English in the community

as everybody started going to school. Her younger siblings never learned the language as she had. George-Hill did not use her native language much for many years, but recently she has been working hard to remember some of the vocabulary that she lost over those years. She recognizes how much harder it is for Indians who didn't grow up in the language.

> *It is really hard for young Indian people nowadays. They feel like it's really hard to learn their language and they're being pulled in two different directions. The only way I learned it is having to be Indian everyday, be around people that speak it. I know there were times when I just didn't speak the language at all, for the longest time. I think probably my junior high and high school years I was so concentrated on trying to be at that grade level because they tell you you have to have 2.0 or better to move onto the next grade so I think during that time I just didn't even really concentrate on my language and I was just trying to get my homework in and just ... I moved the other direction, I guess, I wanted to finish my education. Probably when I went to the Longhouse during the ceremonies, that's when I would hear the language again. I'd get reminded. ... I was the oldest and that's just where it kinda stopped. My other siblings, they don't speak the language, I'm the only one in my family that speaks my language.*

Today, the native-language proficiency among young people is highest on the Fort McDermitt Reservation in the isolated southeastern corner of the state. But even there, people are starting to notice a decline. Younger people are more apt to understand, but not speak, Northern Paiute. Karen Crutcher talked about being angry that her parents didn't push her to learn the language. Now she can usually understand, but she cannot respond back in the language. This stage of "passive bilingualism" in the second generation can lead to complete language loss in the third generation if people are not vigilant.

All languages change constantly, but some change faster than others. Those that are unwritten or that have no standardized form generally change the fastest. Fort McDermitt residents described to us a dialect difference between the Paiute spoken by older and younger residents. The older Paiute was depicted as grammatically more complex and spoken much faster. Rose Curtis talked about the embarrassment of not understanding when elders come up and talk to her at funerals. She has to turn around and ask her aunt, "What did they say?" Speakers of other Oregon languages also indicated to us that the language spoken by younger people was not the same as the language spoken by the elders.

Documentation from earlier times presents evidence of language change as well. In 1929 the Nez Perce Archie Phinney wrote to Franz Boas, "I encounter words and usages very frequently that have become obsolete to the younger generation of the tribe."[3] Mildred Quaempts spoke of a different sort of linguistic difference between the generations. She remembered what expert speakers the elders were and how they made stories come alive by taking on different voices. Today's speakers sound flat to her. Phinney alluded to this same verbal artistry inherent in Indian storytelling and how it is lost when recording the tales in writing.

> *A sad thing in recording these animal stories is the loss of spirit—the fascination furnished by the peculiar Indian vocal rendition for humor. Indians are better storytellers than whites. When I read my story mechanically I find only the cold corpse.*[4]

Human language is the most complex form of communication we know. Knowing a language means knowing a sound system, knowing how words are created, knowing how sentences are organized, knowing the relationships between sounds and meanings and how meanings are ordered into worldviews. But it is also knowing how to use language in attractive, creative ways that make people want to listen to you.

Language change is not necessarily evidence that the language is slipping away, as long as the younger speakers continue to put effort into language development. Unfortunately, several people also reported to us that they were afraid of being laughed at if they made a mistake speaking their Native language. The self-consciousness of adolescents and adults works against language maintenance and revitalization. It leads to the situation where a bilingual generation is followed by a passive bilingual generation whose members understand but don't speak the non-dominant language. This generation is commonly followed by a generation that is monolingual in the dominant language.

Discovering Our Languages

Teachers of Oregon languages today did not have the language wrenched away from them as did previous generations. One group was exposed to lots of fluent Native speech when they were children, but after attending school stopped speaking the language regularly.

Another group (mostly younger) heard only a few words growing up but spent a good part of their adult life trying to attain fluency. Both groups went through a process of discovery. The first group experienced a slow erosion of speakers of the language and places where it was spoken and soon found themselves in a monolingual English environment, except for, perhaps religious ceremonies. Their discovery consisted of realizing the value of something that they had taken for granted. As Mildred Quaempts put it:

> *I wasn't in that generation that dealt with all that harshness of takin' the language away. I was at a point where I was just one of the only ones who could talk and kids from our own tribes were makin' fun of me 'cause I could talk. I didn't realize that I had that treasure with me.*

The second group of teachers grew up in English-dominant households and never gave any thought to ancestral multilingualism. Here Native Americans are no different from the numerous Euro-American young people who have no knowledge that their ancestors immigrated here speaking languages other than English. Radine Johnson sums up her discovery as follows:

> *I didn't even know that there was, that my grandma had a language, until I heard her speaking it at the museum.*

She begins the sentence with a more general statement about the existence of Kiksht, but shifts mid-sentence to a more personal connection to the language. It was her grandma's language and she heard it for the first time in a museum—a place that is designed to showcase things of the past. Yet here was her grandma speaking a language in the present that was unknown to her. This intrigued her enough that she set out to learn more about it.

Other people involved in teaching and learning Oregon Native languages today were in contact with older relatives who spoke "Indian" as they commonly called it. We asked these people when they became aware of multilingualism in their families. Sonny Ryan, who grew up in Wisconsin, remembers his father speaking Chinuk Wawa on the phone to friends and relatives back home at Grand Ronde. Since Ryan never heard anyone else speak the language, he thought it was his dad's own language, not that it belonged to a whole group of people. Other people remembered expressions of their grandparents that they roughly understood without being able to say where one word ended and another began. Everything that a child is surrounded by becomes normal and natural to that child, whether it's the acceptance of someone speaking an entirely different language that they don't fully understand or whether borders between languages are blurred as occurs in code-switching and borrowing. Randee Sheppard recounted the following anecdote about how she discovered that *waw'aaks*, which refers to the dried mucus that accumulates in the corner of your eye, was not an English word. This realization came about when she was sitting around talking with a group of non-Indian friends from high school. She used the word and her friends looked at her quizzically and asked what it meant.

> *"It's the eye goobery stuff in your eye right here," and I used it and no one knew what I was saying. Yeah and I thought that's what everyone used. "Well, that's not what I call it." "Well, I thought it was eye boogers." "'Eye boogers,' what is that?" "Well, I call it sleepy eye," and a bunch of other bogus names came out. Okay, well, I will stick with mine.*

Multilingualism enhances people's ability to consciously examine language. It is only in contrast with another language that we are able to see how our own structures our way of perceiving the world. Language can also be a significant part of our identity and it is often in multilingual settings that children come to the realization that languages are not randomly distributed, but are rooted in particular families. Here is how Stephanie Ohles became interested in her family's languages in metropolitan Portland.

> *In Portland—a lot of Klamaths, Modocs, and Paiutes live there—a lot of my dad's friends live there and he lived there for years, so we ran into them and they'd talk Indian and say rough things in Indian. It was Indian-English-Indian-English and I didn't know what tribe it was; I just knew that my parents understood it so that's where I came from. But I didn't start making a distinction until eighth grade, I think. That was the last year we were in Portland and we started running into racial problems with the principal ... that's when I started seein' that we were a little different. People were comin' into the school then that were speaking Korean, speaking Japanese, African languages and I had never seen that before and they were speaking their languages. And I was like "Hey, mom, how much more language do you know?" ... That's when I started asking questions: What are we? Who are we? Where do we belong? That's when my worlds kind*

Dallas Winishut teaching in the elementary school. Photo by Judy Blankenship, courtesy of Northwest Regional Educational Laboratory.

of opened up. ... There was the Russian community movin'
in the eighties, we had a Slavic guy and he could speak his
language. I started makin' distinctions then.

Dallas Winishut, who is now a teacher of Warm Springs Sahaptin, went off to New Mexico after graduating from high school. There he met people of his age who spoke Indian languages. He told the following story about his linguistic awakening.

I only knew a couple, three words here and there in Ichishkiin.
I'll always remember, this Apache girl, she was the leader of
her group, they kinda hang around in groups. And she goes,
she comes up, she's just talking to her friends, or her cousins,
she looks at me and she goes, "How do you say this in your
language?"
　I'm sitting there like, "I don't know."
　And she talks to her friend in Apache language and goes,
"How would you say this in your language?"
　"I don't know."

And finally she looks at me and she goes, "Are you an Indian?"

I says, "Yeah, I'm an Indian."

"Are you sure?"

And I goes, "Yeah."

"Well how come you don't know your language?"

And those words kind of hit harder than a fist. Kind of made me think about it. You know, twenty years old, and those guys are about the same age and they just use their language every day, talking to each other, and it really made me think. And then later on that evening I called back home and I asked my mother, "Well how do you say this in our language?" or "How do you say ...?" I asked her all kinds of questions. And then at the end I go, "How come you didn't teach me the language?" [laughing]

She just kind of hesitated for a while. And I go, "I'm around people that know their language. Some of them are younger, some of them are the same age, some of them are a little bit older, but they all talk to each other in their own native tongue. I kind of feel like an outcast because I don't know." So those words come back hard to me sometimes. I'll always remember them, probably until the day I'm gone. And I just had to come to something like that, you know: "Are you an Indian?" Oh boy.

While Winishut and Styephanie Ohles discovered their ancestral languages through the participation in multilingual communities and a growing sense of their own cultural heritage, another way in which past generations of Native Americans discovered the importance of their languages was through contact with linguists and anthropologists. These researchers, following the salvage model of anthropology, set out to document the languages and cultures of native groups before they "died out." In so doing, they helped a lot of people "discover" their languages. In the process of recording linguistic materials, a few native speakers of those languages were alerted to the importance of maintaining them. The pairing up of researcher and informant caused many native speakers to think about their language in new ways and many of them began writing their language down and consciously teaching it to others.

Thomas Morning Owl told about the effect that linguist and anthropologist Melville Jacobs had on his ancestor, Charlie McKay. McKay worked with Jacobs and developed his own writing system of

Umatilla based on Jacobs'. Morning Owl was told stories about men hanging around the sweat houses, competing with each other to write the most complex word on the walls of the sweat lodge. Fred Hill reported that Uncle Charlie McKay used to write to him in Umatilla when he was away at boarding school. Mildred Quaempts talked about how Uncle Charlie McKay insisted that no one speak English in the home. Morning Owl, Hill, and Quaempts, all close maternal relatives of Charlie McKay, are Umatilla language teachers today. Another close maternal relative of McKay, Phil Cash Cash, is pursuing a Ph.D. in linguistics with a focus on language revitalization.

Due to the unconscious nature of language, the heightened linguistic consciousness that precedes the formation of language programs often comes from an outsider. Even after the salvage paradigm began to falter, there are numerous examples of how linguists working with an indigenous language have sparked the interest of people in the community to revitalize their language. Once language programs get started, community language activists take on this role. Nowadays, it is more likely that the outsider is from another Native group working on their own language. The role of Hawaiians and Maoris in this process of discovery cannot be underestimated. They are the farthest ahead in the area of language revitalization with university-level students able to carry out intellectual pursuits in the languages of their ancestors.

Remembering/Learning Our Languages

After many years of not speaking a language, it fades away. People who have learned languages in school have experienced this, but it is not quite the same as when that language was your first language: the language in which the people you loved most in the world spoke to you. Many people experience great sadness when they realize what they have lost and great happiness when they begin the process of remembering.

Language is contextualized. It is embodied in stories and experiences. Words and expressions with emotional content are more easily remembered than neutral words.

Janice George-Hill, teacher of Umatilla, talked about how she learned the language through stories and how that has helped her remember it.

> I think that's another way we learned, listening to the kut-lahs
> or the al-ahs, which you know, both mean "grandmothers,"
> but from the paternal and maternal and the pushas and tillas,

Fred Hill, Sr. and Jimmy
Freeman working on
language lessons

*which means "grandfather" both maternal and paternal
and that's how they told stories and that's how I remembered
some of the words because they told us stories in the native
language.*

Of course, it is difficult to maintain a language if there is no one
left to speak it with. Many speakers of Oregon Native languages
found themselves in exactly this position. People moved away from
the community and between school, work, and raising families
eventually found themselves in an all-English environment. Language
revitalization began with trying to locate remaining speakers of the
languages. This is not a straightforward process. Some people doubted
their own abilities; others saw no reason to help out the program for
various reasons. We owe the deepest gratitude to the people who
stepped forward to assist the fledgling programs. Many of these
people had not spoken the language regularly in years and, coming
together, they began the process of remembering. Two elders at Warm
Springs have been reconstructing the Wasco or Kiksht language. I
asked Deanie Johnson who was working with them: "So how many
fluent speakers of Kiksht remain?" She replied, "You're looking at
them." "Just the two of you?" I asked the two elderly women across
the table. "Just the two of us," they replied.[5]

Both women had spent most of their adult lives not speaking
the language they had spoken as children. Getting involved in the
language program has allowed them to bring the language back into
their consciousness and have quite a good time doing so. One of the
elders described the process:

*We kind of, we remembered it getting back together. That's
how we got back into our language. ... We'd remember
something, and say, "Oh, this is how you say it!" But that's*

*how we got our language back. Because we knew it when
we were little, when we were young. My mother and my
grandmother didn't speak English. They spoke the Kiksht
language.*

The pleasure that these elders experienced bringing the language
back into consciousness was also described by Gilbert Towner:

*We have a word list now, and I'll come to one word, and I'll
remember something else that goes along with that word, and
then it kind of builds a picture, and it's a lot of fun to describe
that the best I can in English, and then say the words. And
I'll remember when I was little, a lot of these words will start
coming back to me. It's a lot of fun.*

One word jogs the memory and other words follow. These words
bring back images of past experiences. Just being in particular
environments can also bring forth the language. Language and
experience interconnect, one bringing forth the other. The Native
language program office ideally becomes a gathering place for elder
speakers. They meet there regularly and go over old documentation
of the languages. They listen to tapes, read materials, help with
transcription, and translate back and forth between languages. They
talk about things they learned from their elders. They go on fieldtrips
and explain how materials and food were gathered and processed.
All these sessions are recorded, so that they can be revisited at a later
time. But it is very time-consuming to transcribe and archive these
recordings and while elder-speakers are still alive the emphasis is
on gathering the information. The breaking of natural transmission
has made the remaining speakers into a limited resource and younger
generations are hungry for their wisdom.

Many of the teachers of Oregon Native languages today were not
fluent speakers of the language when they were young. Most of them
grew up hearing words here and there, but at some point decided that
it was important for them to learn the language of their ancestors.
The lucky ones were able to be paired with fluent elders in master-
apprentice programs. Ohles explained how Neva Eggsman got a
group of apprentices started with five words a day and then moved
on to sentences. Ohles described the experience:

*She could talk us down all she wanted to, but she wasn't like
that, she was nice. But she would throw sentences out there
and just laugh because she was watching us trying to figure
out what she was saying and when we started getting it she*

just got prouder and she would give us harder stuff and she'd talk longer in the language but she wanted us to be at a certain place before she'd do that and we were getting there before she got sick. Yeah, it was cool. She'd sit there and just talk in like phrases, like a solid couple sentences. And you're talking about going down to the store and getting some eggs and you ran into your ... son and he just wanted to talk your head off and, you know, you start putting them in and it's like all these words come in and they just fall into place and you see all these words that she taught you and you're just like, "Oh my god, I understand what you just said to me." And it was cool 'cause the words started coming in.

Ohles worked as an apprentice for five years before Eggsman passed away in 2002. Previously, Ohles had wanted to become an artist, but she came to realize that language is a form of art. "It's painting with words and attitude." She also spoke of it as giving her a completeness and making her whole.

Tony Johnson learned Chinuk Wawa through a self-styled master-apprentice program, insisting on speaking it with elders. When he and Henry Zenk became fluent, they took over the "master" role for the next group of students.

You have maybe one place in the world that immersion is available and often in the case of a language like this it's just a few homes and a few ninety-year-old people or eighty-year-old people. So we really have to create environments to make fluent second-language speakers like myself. We really modeled it after what a few people did in California. There is a real movement of using what's there (in California) and that is pairing people who want to learn the language with fluent first-language speakers and you can do anything. You can put these people together and have them do anything. I mean they can be playing basketball together or they can be chopping wood for the elder or washing their dishes or cooking. The point is you have two people, one the language learner and one teacher, and both of them commit only to one thing and that is doing everything they would normally do but through the medium of their native language. It's called "Master-Apprentice," that's what they coined it, and so we've done something like that too ... Now we've trained two people who are my primary teachers up there in the preschool. We have trained them through a real intensive sort

of Master-Apprentice program where they were first exposed
to the elders and then to ourselves. Anyway we tried to do
everything that we did together at work or whatever in Chinuk
Wawa.

Since Chinuk Wawa developed as a creole language, its grammatical
structure is simpler than the other indigenous languages of the state.
This has made the achievement of fluency by adult learners easier.
Learners of other languages have expressed concern about their level
of fluency in the language they are expected to teach. Learning a
language is a long process that takes years of conscious effort if one
does it as an adult. Even a child with a brain that is hardwired to
acquire a language absorbs the sounds and patterns of the language for
a couple years before talking. For the adult learner just producing the
correct sounds can be a nearly insurmountable problem. Becoming a
fluent speaker after one's unconscious language-acquisition device in
the brain has become devoted to other types of knowledge is not an
easy task. It requires a lot of personal interest and many, many hours
of exposure. Since we have become such a monolingual society,
there is a lack of understanding of what the process entails and it
can get very frustrating for language learners. Neva Eggsman, who
instructed apprentices for years in the Klamath language, understood
the difficulty of learning a language as an adult because she had done
it. Her first language was Modoc, but she married a Klamath man
and had to learn to communicate with his mother in Klamath. Her
youngest apprentice, Randee Sheppard, voiced her frustration with
people who expected fluency too soon.

> *They don't understand that we are trying and we are working*
> *really hard to try and become as fluent as they want us to be.*
> *But we can't do it overnight, and they expect it in one year.*
> *And Neva always told us that it took her fifty-five years to*
> *become as fluent as she was, so I mean this is not an overnight*
> *progress thing that we can just wake up tomorrow morning*
> *and we are all fluent, and know what's going on.*

Neva Eggsman, of course, had the advantage of having a fluent,
monolingual speaker in the home. Very few families in Oregon use a
Native language in the home anymore. Young people today must make
a much greater effort to consciously learn the language. Despite the
added barriers, we interviewed several young people who are taking
advantage of lessons offered by the various language programs in
the state. The twelve-year-olds we interviewed at Jefferson County

Middle School had been taking Ichishkiin (Warm Springs Sahaptin) classes since kindergarten. They were aware that they were losing fluent speakers and wanted to learn it and teach it "so that our language wouldn't die." While they don't have the advantage of being brought up with native speakers, they are extremely interested in learning the languages of their ancestors, which they regard as an important part of their identity, and carrying it on to the next generation. Fourteen-year-old Jimmy Freeman in Umatilla put it very nicely:

> *I usually don't see any kids in [the language program office] and I wanna learn this language. When all the* kut-lahs *and* tillas *pass away I wanna be the one that's gonna read it and kinda be speakin' in the future ... And why I want to speak this is to make my family proud. Because my mom wasn't raised Indian 'cause like back then my grandma was Indian but my grandpa he was not recognized from this tribe. He was Seminole. And my mom said back then there was only Indians and Whites and my grandpa chose White.*

Leslie Riggs, aged thirty-six, echoed the same feeling of disconnect with his Indian culture. He talked about becoming more politically aware as he learned about Native American history. Now he feels learning the language is an integral part of this process.

> *I always knew that I had Indian blood but just because I wasn't raised by my father I was pretty much disconnected from the whole thing and I got interested in it sort of at an early age but then I moved to England and then when I got enrolled in the tribe I thought, "Well being a tribal member means more than just getting a per capita check." To me, to*

Umatilla adult
language class

*be a member of the tribe I think that you need to do certain
things. There is a lifestyle involved and language is a big part
of that. So to me it just seems like the right thing to do, I guess.*

We interviewed several adult students of Oregon Native languages.
Some of them worked for the tribes and were given time off to study
their languages. Others were taking it for independent college credit
and others still were just taking time to learn because they felt that it
was important for them to do so. They felt that it connected them with
a place and with their elders. Tina Montoya had this to say:

*It's where I come from and it sounds pretty and I like the
way the old people talk. I wanna be able to understand what
they're sayin ... But when people talk about it I can just see
it in their faces that they're tellin' me more than what I'm
hearing.*

Montoya is describing here the stage of language learning when
you begin to get the gist of conversations, but the subtleties still
escape you. The desire to be able to understand is a strong motivator
to continue learning the language. This can be said for all languages,
but when the people whom you are trying to understand are your own
elders and they possess traditional ecological knowledge about how
your ancestors lived on this land, the motivation is even stronger.

Louis Scott, who works with the Natural Resources department at
Warm Springs, first became aware of wanting to learn the language
when his department began collecting oral histories. They contacted
elders to tell them about Celilo Falls, Willamette Falls, root-digging
areas, and other places that were important to Natives in the past. He
discovered that a lot of the elders were more comfortable in Ichishkiin
than in English.

*The set of interviews that we were trying to develop at that time
were relating to the language lessons. We interviewed families,
the eldest male and eldest female, and how they lived, then the
next generation as it came down, and what was being passed
down; the hunting, the fishing, the beadwork, the traditional
preparing of foods. They were being passed down, but as the
interviews progressed, what was being lost was the language.
There was one generation that knew it, and the next one didn't,
and our generation, or my generation didn't, don't know it. So,
that was the result of the series of interviews that we had done
at that time ... I think everybody was at a loss. You see an elder,
and you understand their knowledge, and then to see them pass*

on, you know that it's gone forever. So that was a major, I guess, a set-back with the language. In working with the senior citizens even makes it more relevant, when you see a person there, and they're gone maybe the next month. So you understand the loss, the loss is really, really great.

Another theme that emerged among learners in their twenties and thirties was the desire to pass the language on to their children. They recognized that they were not given the chance to learn the language as children and wanted to try to offer that opportunity to their own children. Earlier home-based language lessons were meant to engage the entire family in the language-learning experience. These were well received when the children in the family were young, but American children soon develop their own activity agendas and language lessons in the home were outrun by the competition. The Grand Ronde tribe has built on the desires of parents of young children by forming an immersion preschool in Chinuk Wawa. In order for children to be accepted into the program, their parents must sign a contract that they will take lessons themselves, participate in immersion events, and speak to their children fifteen minutes a day in the language. When we visited this program, three-year-olds were speaking to each other in Chinuk Wawa on the playground—a sign that the language had taken hold in their minds. They were beyond the repetition stage and were making up new sentences, even creating new words based on other Chinuk Wawa roots.

All of these students had some local Indian background, but we also talked with a man of Mexican background who worked for the Warm Springs tribe who was studying Sahaptin. Being brought up

Teaching the three languages of Warm Springs at a Natural Resources Day Presentation

bilingually in English and Spanish, he saw the value in learning new languages and gaining new perspectives. He practiced the language with his girlfriend's parents and said that they were quite pleased. We also talked with other Euro-Americans who were studying Chinuk Wawa. They were all native Northwesterners who felt a strong connection to the land where they were raised and sensed that learning a native language was the right thing to do. Some were concerned about the dying off of languages, but most spoke of an organic connection between the land and the language that developed on that land.

Teaching our Languages

One of the reasons Bobby Mercier thinks that his great-aunt, Eula Petite, was able to implement Chinuk Wawa lessons in the local public school in the 1960s was because it was spoken by many of the Euro-Americans living in the area, so it had already developed as a non-racialized Northwest identity marker, dialect differences notwithstanding. Petite was one of the earliest teachers of an Oregon native language in the school system. She taught in the old agency school at Grand Ronde and developed a Chinuk Wawa curriculum that is used to this day.

Other people we talked with remembered efforts to consciously teach Native languages beginning in the 1970s, post-Civil Rights. None of the present programs today date back to that time, however. Different models have been experimented with over time: adult classes, home-based teaching, language and culture camps, master-apprentice programs. Several of the tribal publications include language lessons, a couple of people have made language CDs, new songs are being composed in Klamath and Umatilla, and two of the reservations include some language in a local radio station. More recently, they have added classroom-based programs and (thanks to models from New Zealand and Hawaii) preschool immersion. Warm Springs and Grand Ronde are focusing on early childhood education while Umatilla and Siletz both have new charter high schools. In Nixyaawii on the Umatilla Reservation, students can choose to take Umatilla, Walla Walla, or Nez Perce classes, offered every morning.

I mentioned earlier how a couple of the language teachers today became cognizant of their own ancestral languages when they found themselves in multilingual situations. For example, Dallas Winishut became interested in learning Ichishkiin in the multilingual atmosphere of New Mexico, where young people of his age were speaking their Native languages. Phyllis Walker, a Paiute teacher at

Beatty, talked about first figuring out how to teach her language in the multilingual Stuart Indian school in Nevada. For Walker, knowing how to write the language was instrumental to teaching it and she had never written it down before. She went home and asked her mother and together they figured out a system.

> *I started in school, I guess, really, 'cause I was meeting different tribes at school in Stuart, Nevada. And us girls would get together and some were Shoshone, some were Navajo, you know, different tribes. And then we'd all share words, you know, "How do you say it? How do you write it ...?" Now that's really how we got started. And then I said, "I don't know."—"Well, I don't either." [laughs] So we just kinda wrote it the way it sounded and then I was talkin' to my mom, she was kinda a smart old lady, and then she said—we were tryin' to spell words and I was tellin' her about what we did in school—and she said, "I don't think that's too hard, I think you can do it, just learn those vowels and you'll get it," she told me. She's the one that got me on the vowels. She was a pretty smart old lady.*

When we visited Walker, she brought out a dictionary that she was working on late into the night and a packet of curriculum that she had created along with help from Paiute teachers in Nevada and Warm Springs.

To teach a language, one has to reach another level of consciousness about the language, figuring out how to break it down into learnable segments. Ideally, after attaining the basic grammatical structure and vocabulary of a language, the learner can spend an extended period of time in an immersion environment. This is much easier to do if you are learning a language that still has monolinguals interacting in the language. These environments are increasingly scarce in the Native communities of Oregon. The language program at Umatilla has tried to recreate immersion situations with mixed success. In the end, the Longhouse turned out to be the most natural place. Mildred Quaempts spoke of the difficulty of finding spaces where people can focus on the language without external distractions.

> *We talk about immersion, but it's really hard because of our setting. We have too much going on, there's always a car goin' by with a radio on, newspapers and everything in front of us. I could go home and I almost have to have one empty space. Well, I guess the best space is the Longhouse, we speak a lot of the language there.*

With elders becoming frailer and less suited for the energetic work of teaching children, tribes have asked younger people to step forward to become teachers. Most of these people feel like they don't know enough to teach the language. It's an uncomfortable position for younger people to be teaching languages of which they know far less than their elders. A couple of the teachers we interviewed talked about their reluctance to take on this role and their "baptism by fire." Radine Johnson put it this way:

> *I was working at Extension, and Val worked across the hall, and she just came in one day and said, "We need a, you should apply for the teacher position, of the Kiksht language." And I just started, grandma started living with me, and I'd bring her up for her classes, and I'd sit in class, so I was getting involved in that, and then I didn't feel like I knew enough to become a teacher, and I told Val, "The next time it comes open, I'll apply, but not now," not thinking that it would come open again. So a year later it did, and so I had to keep my promise and apply, and so I started work, and I went to class on my first day, I went to class with Val over at the grade school. And the second day I was teaching.*

Winishut explained the difficulty of trying to become fluent in the language at the same time that you are teaching it.

> *Being more fluent in our Ichishkiin language, that's my biggest challenge right now. I'm working on it. But it's good because I've got two fluent, three fluent speakers ... Well, even like the archives that were left behind from the other teachers, a lot of them are just kind of incomplete. ... And that's what I was just doing, I was looking for our archives on things that I want to teach, like making nets, making a sweathouse, cultural things that I can teach younger boys ... That's what I want to start teaching. In order to do that, I want to learn it better, and I want to be able to keep it in the language when I teach it, and so that's what I'm really looking forward to, and that's always going to be a challenge, I believe, because the material isn't there. I mean, maybe it is, I just need to really research harder, and have more time to research.*

The line between being a teacher and being a student is a flexible one. Just as teachers are simultaneously students, students can also be teachers. Many students practice the language with younger siblings, for instance. Jess Nowland is a very serious student of Nez Perce. In addition to spending two hours a week in classes, he devotes between two and eight hours per week creating study projects, word lists, games, etc. in that language. He has created jeopardy questions, pyramids, word searches, and crossword puzzles in Nez Perce. Then he plays these games with the other students who come to class. Nowland says that people learn more when they're playing than when they are just expected to memorize words.

All the people we interviewed find teaching a challenging task. All of them were chosen for the classroom because of their language abilities and interest, not because they had teaching experience. Being faced with a room full of single-aged children for a short period of time during which they are supposed to learn something is not a situation that most people are faced with in daily life. Teaching is not an easy enterprise when the students are not especially motivated to learn. Some kids see no purpose in learning another language as long as "everyone speaks English." There is also a problem with introducing a language when people are at their most self-conscious stage—teenagerhood. It's often difficult to get teenagers to practice the language out loud because they think it will tarnish their image. A Paiute teacher in McDermitt, Betty Krutcher, was having trouble with a high school class and she asked an outspoken elder to come and help her one day. The elder went once and didn't make much headway. The next time she was asked, she came up with a new idea. Her granddaughter, Jane Crutcher, told this account:

> *She'd been there once before and she thought, "Well, that didn't work so now I'm gonna show 'em something else." She has this dog. He's not really big, he's got a long body and it's a mixed breed and she speaks Paiute to the dog—"Go lay down, go sit down ..." And that dog understood Paiute. She said, "I know what I'm gonna do—I'm taking my dog to school." So I came and picked her up and we went and Betty said, "Well, what're you gonna tell my students today?" So she brought her dog in. And I was just sitting there watching her and she went over there and she spoke in Paiute the whole time she was there. And she told 'em, "That's the only way you're gonna learn. You walk in that door you start speaking Paiute once you get in the class." Anyway she spoke Paiute to her dog, "C'mere, lay down, sit up ..." you know, all these commands that anybody would give to their dogs, the last one really got me. I didn't know she could do this, she made her dog roll over, she made him stand up on his hind legs and turn around. And it was all in Paiute. Then he sat down and she*

told those kids, "I brought my dog to show you that if he can understand, you can too and you can speak it and if my dog could speak he'd tell you!"

Jane Crutcher's grandmother was demonstrating that any language could be adapted to serve any purpose and that there wasn't anything intrinsically unlearnable about Northern Paiute. They just needed exposure and practice.

Unlike teachers of most subjects taught in school, teachers of Native Oregon languages have to come up with their own curriculum. Some language programs have been working on this for several years, but there is a need for more, age-appropriate, interesting materials in all the language programs. For Arlita Rhoan, a veteran teacher of Ichishkiin, this is her biggest challenge.

Teaching material, you know we have to make our own, and it's always just, not real good ... there's a lot of work that needs to be done, you have to make up material that somebody else behind us will be able to use. So we have to do a lot of work like that. And that's a challenge, because we're teaching at the same time.

Linguists who have been working on the issue of language endangerment have developed guidelines that help move along the process of revitalization. Writing the language down, using electronic technology to spread the language, and increasing its presence within

Arlita Rhoan teaching in the elementary school. Photo by Judy Blankenship, courtesy of Northwest Regional Educational Laboratory.

the local education system are some of the ways that have proved successful in this venture.⁶ However, the brutal history of colonization has left its mark on speakers of Native languages, who often feel like their language is the one thing that Euro-Americans have not been able to take from them. Because of this, some speakers are against writing the language down, even though written languages are far more likely to survive in our highly literate world than ones that are only orally transmitted. They resist using writing and electronic technology to disseminate the language, not knowing who might be capturing it. There is a fairly widespread belief in Native communities that one's language was a sacred gift of the Creator. This is interpreted by some as a linguistic pact between the supernatural being and a particular group of humans who learn the language naturally in their families. The idea of carving the language up into manageable segments and artificially teaching it to people strikes them as irreverent. It also leads many elders to reason that the language should definitely not be taught to those outside the tribe, or sometimes even to those within the tribe who don't follow traditional ways. This has been interpreted in a different way by Gilbert Towner, who is intent on revitalizing Tututni, a language that was declared extinct a few decades ago:

> *I think to myself that the Creator gave us our language for free. Who am I to say that you couldn't try to learn the language too? It's not up to me to say, who is there and who is not. If they are interested in the language, I'm there to try to teach.*

Breathing Life Back into Our Languages

Languages like most sorts of knowledge begin to fade once people cease using them, so it is important that people continue using what they learn. Mildred Quaempts has a vision of children being immersed in the language without disruptions in English. "We want them to hear and understand and be able to converse with us in their Native language." She urges her students to be "fearless" about speaking the language. She tells them not to be afraid to speak it and not to feel bad when they're corrected by their elders. "I tell them that it's up to them to pass the language along to the next generation. They will be elders, too, someday."

Much of the curriculum in Native languages is based on long-established ways of life, and carries a lot of traditional ecological knowledge. Students learn about digging roots, gathering berries, fishing, hunting, basket weaving, food preparation and preservation, among other things. They learn about these activities as they learn the Native language. But the teachers realize that the world the students live in is not the same as that of their ancestors, so they also learn to tell time and what to call telephones and computers. All teachers want the subjects that they teach to be meaningful and useful to their students. Native language teachers are even more concerned than most that their students carry the language on and teach it to others, not only because the language is endangered, but because it is integrally intertwined with a way of seeing the world that is equally at risk. Janice George-Hill put it this way:

> *I was hoping that all our classes, all our time that we spend with different people who are willing to learn, that they'll be able to retain the language and use it and teach it and I'm hoping that our language will never fade ... There are songs that we sing that have a lot to do with our way of life here on Earth and help us get ready for when we come to the end of our life; you know it's a cycle that is taught to us that we always have to be like ready for anything that comes along and the language has a lot to do with being prepared for anything that comes along and anything, food gathering, the name giving, even when a person passes on, everything that we do, the language mixes in with it. It's more important to use the language and it has a better meaning to everything that we do and it's more meaningful when we speak in the language. It's our way of life.*

Perhaps Native languages have a sacred aura to them because they have remained most vibrant in the sacred realm. Fred Hill talked about how important it is to pray in the Native language and how people are often drawn into learning the language through the Native religion. In this way Native languages are similar to Hebrew and Arabic with their connection to Judaism and Islam respectively. Hill called the songs "messages to us from our Creator" and described how in listening to them and singing them "we are straightened out in our minds and hearts to live right." He expressed this sacred connection in a beautiful manner.

> *When we sing our language songs in our religion, those are prayers. Even though they're very old, they're kept fresh and new when they're brought up whenever the time is. Sometimes it's like, if we've been away from it awhile, sometimes the songs come out real strong and they sound real beautiful. It's like drinking real good spring water.*

The spiritual has close connections with environmental problems we are experiencing today. Stephanie Ohles feels that everyone should learn about tribal culture to avoid cultural misunderstandings. She commented on the ongoing struggles in the Klamath Basin when asked about the importance of teaching Native language and culture.

They don't know why we're so upset about the water. They don't know why we're so upset about irrigating and chemicals in the earth. We're talking about generations of people that still remember when the river was high and full of bags of fish. That's all you could see was fish, fish, fish, fish. It wasn't dammed, it wasn't dirty, it was clear without moss, you didn't have to worry about dead cows floating down it and now you do. They give you warnings not to swim in it. It's rugged, it's nasty. Now there's so much algae. Well, if they quit irrigating and putting the fertilizer in the land that leaches into the water and they dredge the Klamath Lake just so they can have a ferry run through ... So if they were educated about our tribe and the surrounding tribes, the original foods and places they live in, why they gathered this and why they lived this way and why they're separated and why they had the war, then they would start understanding.

Tony Johnson also praised the wisdom of his ancestors, who could accurately predict the weather. He marveled at the fact that they described the earth as a round blue and green ball in their creation myth, long before images taken from space revealed it to be so. He stressed that the Chinook were telling this story when Europeans still thought the world was flat.

Just the smallest little thing, if you are on the north shore of the Columbia River and the sun rises and you can see Saddle Mountain, you know that it is going to be a clear day, the day will be clear. That's a fact. And that's something that we've made over ten thousand years of looking across the river. There may be a scientific way to look at it but the point is it's been known by our ancestors. I really like those things ... that we have really known to be facts or have really slick old stories about, because you know we kind of try and make fun of the fact that Europeans thought the world was flat because our oldest story (without all the details) talks about the sun being so lonely and just being there, she's just there, and then wishing for a companion, seeing finally this little round grey marble. It looked just like a perfectly round stone and so she started breathing on this out in the distance and breathed life into it and it was all this vibrant color blue and green. It was our earth. We have many versions of the story before there was ever anybody that went out in space and looked at the earth and knew what it looked like.

One clear connection between language and the environment is place names. The Confederated Tribes of Umatilla recently completed a map of their territory using the Native names for places. Jess Nowland said that he thought place names were better described in Indian languages. He told us that many of the place names go back to Coyote stories. In other words, the oral literature of the tribe is inscribed on the landscape.

It kinda goes back to what I was talking about when we pray. That's a connection that people have to this area, we pray in the language that was given to us by the Creator and that includes it all ... the Earth is part of that, a big part of the religion: the Earth, the animals, the plants. But if you look at some of the place names, too, like over towards Walla Walla they have a place called noosh-nu-pa which is talkin' about a place that looks like a nose and that's the shape that the river takes right there, I mean the river looks just like a nose. So that's a good example, it's more than just a place name like "Dayton" or named after somebody, it's actually a characteristic of the earth and the way that the water is moving, I think that it's really not that big of a deal but I think those kind of things could easily be preserved by using the Indian languages rather than the English. 'Cause we all know the English names of these places by now, all the signs and maps that are all marked out in the English language, but we don't see that kind of thing in the Indian language at least not 'til now, we're developing a place name atlas for this area. But I think it's a part of our identity to recognize these places and if you're doing research about family or the people who live in this area and all the oral histories that we've recorded and interviews like the one that we're doing now, they refer to a lot of those places in the Indian language but when they talk about one place, they'll talk about it in the Indian language, then they'll say it's over near Dayton or its over near LaGrande, some of 'em don't exactly coincide with the English names, it could be miles and miles apart. I think

*that's for a purpose too, some of those places, like, are at the
mountain and are secluded and that's how you can really zero
in and understand what they were talking about, because there
was no English place name for the area between LaGrande
and Indian Lake so you almost have to use Indian to describe
where you're talking about.*

At the McDermitt Reservation, Derek Hinkey, who worked in
natural resources, told us that many of the old-timers only knew the
Indian names for places. Several misunderstandings had taken place
between Euro-Americans and Indians who were using different names
for the same place. Jane Crutcher told us that the name of one of the
local mountains translated as "warm" or "hot." In the winter when all
the mountains are snow-capped, this one has very little snow, if any.

Other cultural habits are embedded in the languages as well.
Nowland talked about how it was easier to talk about body parts
in Nez Perce, because in English certain body parts are considered
obscene:

*Especially the "private" areas of the body. In English it
almost seems like you're cussing or you're talkin' dirty but in
Nez Perce it doesn't seem that way. It's almost more natural, I
guess. You're not ashamed to say those words in Nez Perce but
for some reason in English it feels uncomfortable and I think it
has something to do with the public school system and the way
that we were taught. In elementary school, at the time I went
to school, you could get in trouble for saying words that dealt
with the private areas with the body but in Nez Perce, there
are no cuss words.*

As we can see by the examples above, languages are intimately
related to life. Native language teachers do not see themselves as
teaching an intellectualized subject that has little to do with the day-
to-day lives of children. They see themselves firstly as teachers, as
people who have had the privilege of learning to speak their language
from their elders and who have the desire to pass on wise teachings
that can improve the lives of their people. They are painfully aware
that many of their students do not come from strong, stable families
and that drug and alcohol abuse has negatively affected family
relations. Some struggle with their Indian identity. Almost everyone
has multiple ethnic groups represented in their background, but society
likes to classify people as belonging to one group or another. Mildred
Quaempts told one adolescent of mixed heritage who was wondering

what language he should learn: "It's whatever moves in your heart, whatever language you want to learn, you can talk English, Spanish, Umatilla ... but what would be really cool is how about learning all those languages?"

Arlita Rhoan incorporates a lot of lessons about living in the proper manner while she teaches Ichishkiin and she has seen it have a good effect on her students. When teaching body parts, for example, she talks about the importance of taking good care of our bodies. She stresses that no matter what hardships her students might have had, they have their own bodies to work with and they must always take the right path. "Ichishkiin has helped them, because they're finding identity. And eventually, pretty soon they're going to think, 'Well, I'm not going to live that way, the way I was brought up. I'm going to do better for myself.'"

Conclusion

The blatant effort by the American government to obliterate Native American culture and language and later societal pressures to conform were met with resistance. Using the forbidden language, running away from boarding school, and keeping one's sacred traditions secret from Euro-American society are all forms of resistance that have helped maintain the languages that were targeted for destruction. To this day, the sacred domain is the one in which indigenous languages are the strongest. Many people find their way back to the language through sacred activities.

Positive resistance is what allowed the Native languages to survive in the center of some Indian families throughout the time when they were under attack in the public sphere. We must not forget that the maintenance of native languages in Oregon occurred through the conscious effort of a few devoted families and individuals who, in spite of the rising tide against their language and culture, continued speaking their mother tongues and following some of their traditional ways. Many linguists and anthropologists recorded Native languages at the end of the nineteenth and the beginning of the twentieth centuries, and this documentation has been very helpful for people today who are revitalizing their languages; but the purpose of this documentation was to "save" the languages for science, not for the people who developed and used them. The proof is that many of these partially recorded languages have died out entirely, leaving us only with the written documents of one or two researchers.

The people who continued speaking their languages and those who recorded the languages deserve our appreciation, but in terms of current language revitalization, we must appreciate the efforts of the teachers and students of Oregon Native languages today. The path they have chosen is not an easy one. Other languages are far easier to pronounce and their grammatical systems are more like that of English. Other languages have centuries of written literature to draw from and generations of teaching materials adapted to learners of all ages. These people are, in many cases, starting from scratch, but with an incredible desire to do something important for their people and for the world. Stephanie Ohles called it "community work," not "labor," and described her feelings when working with the language:

> *When people call me and ask me, "Can you name my kid?"*
> *I get excited. Or, "We wanna sing this song, or make a*
> *memorial song." "Oh, I got some good words for you." Then*
> *I'll just start rattlin' them off. That gets me excited and I*
> *wanna stay in that. That's where my joy is. When I get up in*
> *the morning, it's the first thing I think about. When I come*
> *home and I'm tired, it's the last thing I think about ... I made*
> *the promise to pass it on as best I can.*

Chapter Three

The Present Climate for Native Language Education

Erin Haynes

Introduction

Though often inconspicuous, language plays an exceedingly important role in every educational program and strategy, from the federal policies that shape curricula to the individual classroom interactions between teachers and students, and every step in between. As the first chapter of this book demonstrated, language was used as a powerful tool for the attempted assimilation of Native Americans, and it continues to be a significant factor in the education of Native American students.

People feel very strongly about language, and about how it should be used to educate the next generation of workers, parents, and leaders in this country. Many aspects of language policy in the public education system are hot political issues. These include which language should be used as the medium of instruction, which languages should be taught as subjects and at what age that instruction should begin, how much classroom time should be invested in language teaching, and how much classroom time should include a non-standard language or dialect as the medium of instruction. Economic concerns include how much money should be spent on language programs and whether to promote monolingualism or bilingualism. While these issues pertain to a wide range of languages and language speakers, the attitudes and ideas that drive them have important consequences for Native American language programs in public schools.

A crucial point here is that linguistic education policy does not happen in a political vacuum, nor is it guided entirely by pedagogical reasoning. Decisions affecting bilingual education methods are strongly influenced by the national values of the time, which in turn inform legislation, educational policy, and Native American language-revitalization efforts. The revival of English-only movements is one current aspect of legislation that is potentially deleterious to language revitalization, and will be discussed later in this chapter. However, other legislation supporting the use of Native American languages in public school has the potential for positive outcomes; using heritage languages improves student self-esteem and achievement, and has wider implications for a group whose languages and cultures have been historically scorned in the United States education system.

The Purpose of Education

Every culture has some form of education, be it in formal classrooms with a single teacher trained for that purpose, in one-on-one relationships between adults and children learning a specific task or trade, or as informal lessons taught to individual or small groups of children as they grow older. Children are trained to participate in the institutions common to the adults of their society, be they vocational, religious, civic, artistic, or otherwise important to the proper functioning of the community. In this way, the community's knowledge and values can be transmitted to the next generation, and children are encouraged to make the transition to adulthood as fully viable and contributing members of their respective communities.

Traditional Native American methods for teaching their children did not involve classrooms with rigid time schedules and standardized tests. The continent of North America contained thousands of communities and cultures, and education varied accordingly, so no single teaching style can be termed "Native American," but in general children were expected to watch others and learn how to properly perform the various tasks pertaining to their future societal responsibilities. Lessons were often oral, and addressed ways of surviving as well as spiritual instruction about people's connection to the earth and its inhabitants. Many other kinds of lessons instructed children about the roles they would play as adults. In many communities, older siblings and cousins undertook some of the child-rearing, and teaching duties were often shared between several older relatives.[1]

As discussed in Chapter One, the coming of European traders and settlers and the establishment of the United States drastically changed these methods of knowledge transmission. The government's goal for Native American children was to "civilize" them. Families were encouraged, coerced, threatened, or otherwise compelled to enroll their children in Western-style schools, where the goal was complete assimilation to the lifestyle of the newly formed nation. Native American children were to learn to subscribe to a Judeo-Christian mode of thinking and abandon their values and traditions, including their languages. The Judeo-Christian tradition continues in America's public schools today, and includes many customs and values that people born into that tradition take for granted, not recognizing its ubiquity in public institutions. For example, in this tradition, the written word is more highly valued than oral speech, and so any piece of information must be backed up with written sources. Trust in written text stems from a reverence for the Bible and belief in its truth in written form.[2] As testimonies from Chapter Two indicate, such adherence to written text and distrust of oral tradition effectively negates Native American perspectives of history.

Education in the United States has become a formal national institution, meaning that it entails an established and widely accepted array of values and actions that are reinforced by positive and negative social sanctions.[3] Historically, this educational institution has had four main purposes: to train children to be good citizens, to train children for a vocation, to forge feelings of nationalistic pride among a diverse group of people, and to provide equal access to resources and opportunities for all Americans.[4] The strength of each purpose in determining current educational laws and practices depends a great deal on public opinion and political trends, with pressure placed on schools to align with public and political shifts in values.[5] This means that the purposes for and methods used in public education change according to national values, and not necessarily because of pedagogical research. School reforms appear, disappear, and reappear according to what is in vogue at a particular time.

During the 1960s and '70s, the national focus on civil rights and equality shaped educational reform that valued students' native languages and reaffirmed their rights to academic success. This focus appears to have changed. Educational researchers over the past decade have remarked on the "nationalistic" attitude that is currently driving education reform. At the Second Annual White House Conference on Character Building for a Democratic, Civil Society in 1995, the Center for Civic Education warned that democracy in this country "faces some daunting challenges," including the idea that ethnic splintering can impair American unity.[6] Though the Center also referred to our ethnic diversity as one of the strengths of our democracy, people have begun to view it as a threat to the tradition of "Americanization" in public schools. They feel that this tradition of assimilation has been a hallmark of the U.S. education system, and some people attribute America's greatness to it.[7] Fears of group "Balkanization" drive reform that excludes languages other than English from public school classrooms.

Nationalism is currently a major factor in shaping education policy, but it is not the only one. Economic concerns also play a role.

It is therefore logical that, in a rapidly expanding global network, education should include a global perspective that emphasizes diversity and critical reasoning so that students can function in an increasingly complex world.[8] This global perspective should include the experiences of Native American students, who represent a historical group that has spanned millennia on this continent. When all students gain an understanding and appreciation of the diversity that surrounds them, they become better able to cope with the large amounts of diversity they will encounter as adults, both in the job market and in their communities.

Two additional factors in determining language policy today are social mobility and equal access. Social mobility, in this context, refers to an individual's ability to use his or her education to help achieve higher socioeconomic power, and equal access is the idea that all people deserve an equal opportunity to acquire the best education for which they have potential.[9] Within the notion of equality in education is the goal of giving children the ability to determine their own futures and identities, or self-determination. All students should gain equal access to the opportunities that await them as adults, and should be able to form their own identities in dialogue with the world around them. This can only be a reality, however, if all students have access to educational materials that reflect their home language and culture. Such materials expand the kinds of choices students can make, and bridge the gap between their traditional culture and the mainstream culture they often encounter at school. They also give children a full range of options from which to form their identities, and allow them to do so without feeling that they must "give up" either their home identity or their school identity.[10]

Both goals of equal access and nationalism are very strong motivators for education policy in the United States, and their interactions drive some of the most hotly contested issues in public education today. As we will see below in our discussion of English-only policies, there is a great deal of controversy over whether students should be encouraged to embrace their heritage languages and cultures as a source of self-worth and identity, or whether they should abandon their backgrounds and assimilate to the dominant culture in order to survive in a global marketplace that favors Western ideals.

In *The Monolingualism of the Other*, an autobiographical account of the painful loss of one's heritage tongue in the wake of colonialism, author Jacques Derrida satirically states,

> *Today, on this earth of humans, certain people must yield to the homo-hegemony of dominant languages. They must learn the language of the masters, of capital and machines; they must lose their idiom in order to survive or live better.*[11]

However, research shows that while mastering the dominant language (or dialect) of a given community allows one certain economic and social privileges, to do so at the cost of losing one's heritage tongue can have damaging effects. In the next two sections, we will discuss the importance of heritage languages for student learning and school achievement.

Fitting a Circular Peg into a Linear Hole

Research suggests that the cultural norms of Native American children contribute to styles of classroom learning that are different from the learning styles of Caucasian students, and that these differences lead to great frustration for Native Americans as they struggle to accommodate their cultural traditions to their teacher's approach to education.[12] As the title of this section suggests, many Native American cultures embrace a circular approach to the world, viewing life as a movement through interconnected circles of time, seasons, and family in repeating cycles. Western culture, on the other hand, views the world in a linear fashion, perceiving time as movement through space in a single direction. This very fundamental difference in perception can contribute to Native American students' frustration in classrooms modeled on Western values. For example, composing essays and stories in a fashion that is expected by their teachers is more difficult when it is different from the style of stories told in their families.

Other cultural differences abound, and though some of them may seem very subtle, they nonetheless greatly affect the ways that different children will approach learning. One example is the fact that American education often strongly emphasizes competition and individual achievement, whereas many Native American students come from cultures where interdependence is emphasized, and competition for individual gain is frowned upon. In these societies, children are discouraged from distinguishing themselves as better than others.[13] Thus teaching styles that emphasize the individual may alienate Native American children who don't want to appear rude by attempting to surpass their peers. In addition, Native American students often prefer visual learning, have a global, holistic, and reflective learning style, and tolerate silence and respect reticence better than their Caucasian peers.[14]

In a study of school-aged children on the Confederated Tribes of Warm Springs Reservation in central Oregon, University of Arizona anthropologist Susan Philips describes specific cultural differences that contribute to the children's underachievement in school.[15] These include different modes of paying attention in class, different ways of interacting with peers, and different reactions to teachers' communicative styles. The Native American children she describes enter the education system with a communicative background well suited to their families and community, but not to the classroom. For example, in normal Warm Springs interactions, each speaker has maximum control over their own turns at speaking. Speakers are not interrupted, and other speakers are not expected to immediately respond to what they have said; each speaker may speak when and for how long they choose, but not in such a way that encroaches on the speaking turns of other people. Philips found that, because of their upbringing, Warm Springs children are much better than their Caucasian peers at large-group interactions and group projects, where no specific person directs conversation. However, they struggle to master appropriate communicative behavior in the standard classroom setting, where one person (the teacher) controls all speech behaviors.

These cultural differences in learning styles are not insurmountable, however, and both tribal knowledge and Western research suggest that introducing Native American language classes into classrooms can help students bridge the gap between home and school expectations. An overwhelming majority of teachers in the state of Oregon are Caucasian and come from a middle-class background.[16] Native language teachers, on the other hand, are almost always members of the tribal community, and thus have a closer cultural connection to their students. Their teaching styles are more likely to match the students' learning styles, and language teachers in the state of Oregon report good behavior and eager learning from their students.[17] Their presence is not only helpful in terms of "cultural brokerage" between Native students and non-Native teachers, but it also lets students know that their community members are validated by the school system. In the next section, we will more closely explore the value of introducing linguistically and culturally relevant curricula into public school classrooms with Native American students.

The Benefits of an Inclusive Education

Learning style differences are not the only challenges that face Native American students in mainstream public classrooms. They also enter a world where their culture and self-identity are brought into question on a daily basis both through the educational materials they encounter and by the general tendency of educational institutions to place a higher value on mainstream modes of thought. The very language of instruction sends a strong message to Native American students about the worth of their heritage; the non-inclusion of the languages spoken by community elders and passed down by their ancestors through thousands of years indicates that their background is not important enough for formal education.[18] Michele Moses, a Professor of Education at the University of Colorado at Boulder, states,

> *Students collaterally learn that their heritage language and culture are inferior to English and the dominant culture. What they should learn instead is that while their heritage language and culture may be different from the U.S. mainstream, both are deserving of respect and recognition.*[19]

However, formal education has been a means of stifling this heritage, and years of assimilatory practices have left their mark on the achievement rates of Native American students. This group has the highest drop-out rate of any racial or ethnic group, and it can be as high as 85 percent in urban high schools.[20] Overall, Native American students have the lowest academic achievement nationally of any ethno-cultural group.[21]

Numerous studies point to the efficacy of including appropriate linguistic and cultural material in classrooms serving minority students.[22] Students are very perceptive to subtle messages telling them that their culture is not appreciated, and they are bombarded with such messages every day in textbooks and curricula that ignore or stereotype their heritage and communities. Even if not explicit, such messages are perpetuated by lessons and texts that promote the dominant culture while downplaying their own.[23] Patrick Burk of the Oregon Department of Education comments, "If students feel alienated, if parents feel ignored, if the environment is hostile, students don't learn." Myra Johnson, Director of the Language Program at the Confederated Tribes of Warm Springs, asserts that a more inclusive education would be good for all students, as it would incorporate more learning styles and give students a broader view of the world in which they live:

*I think it would be beneficial to the schools if they would
be more open to new ideas, new styles of teaching, new
information to be taught. It would not only benefit Native kids,
it would benefit everyone else, and I think there's a real need
for education about who we are.*

Such cultural lessons would be easily incorporated into language
lessons, and including languages in the schools would give students
an opportunity to form a strong connection to their community even
as they learn to operate within dominant society. In this section,
the connections between language, culture, identity, and Native
sovereignty will be explored.

Language and Culture

Culture is what differentiates humans from other species and language
is the primary means by which culture is passed on. This isn't to say
that a culture necessarily disappears when a language ceases to be
spoken. Many Native Americans attend ceremonies and celebrations,
practice traditional arts, music, and religion, and otherwise participate
in their cultural heritage without speaking the language of their
ancestors. Cultural values can be translated into other languages with
more or less difficulty and nonverbal habits form an important part
of culture. Nevertheless, language represents an implicit analysis of
experience. People who speak Native American languages remark
that it encourages them to think in different ways. Tony Johnson, who
is the Cultural Education Coordinator of the Confederated Tribes of
Grand Ronde and runs the Grand Ronde immersion preschool (the
first one in the state of Oregon) put it this way:

*It's just not your blood or whatever else that makes you have
an understanding of your culture, it's language. The things
that our kids say are kind of dumbfounding at times because
they're things that we've only heard from old-time Indians. I
mean, it's a really cool deal for us. There is a lot more built
into this than just the language. It's a different language and it
carries the sensibilities of our elders in it. It's just nice that the
kids are really perceiving it in a natural way. They are in tune
with that much older way of thinking.*

These are the kinds of ideas that preoccupied Edward Sapir, an
anthropologist who worked on Oregon languages in the early years
of the twentieth century. He passed these notions on to his student,
Benjamin Whorf, who asked, "Are our own concepts of 'time,' 'space,'

and 'matter' given in substantially the same form by experience to all men, or are they in part conditioned by the structure of particular languages?"[24] He tentatively answered this question by pointing out how language "shapes" thought. As an example, he called attention to the way in which European languages turn intangibles like time into concrete objects that can be counted, such as minutes, hours, and days. When we think about it, we can see that none of these time categories can be lined up and counted the way we might count apples, but linguistically we can do exactly that. Other languages impede this comparison and instead the cyclical nature of time is more apparent in the structure of the language. What has come to be known as the Sapir-Whorf hypothesis is often overstated as "Language determines thought." Whorf, in fact, did not reduce language solely to its grammatical structure, but contextualized it in patterns of usage which he called "fashions of speaking." Dell Hymes, who worked on Oregon languages several decades after Sapir, continued in this line of thinking. He called for the need to investigate "ways of speaking," which led to the development of the "ethnography of speaking" perspective within linguistic anthropology. This way of conceiving the relationship between language and culture has proved the most fruitful to researchers.

It is therefore important to see language as a social act and as a repertoire of community history and experiences. Though a certain language may not be intrinsically linked to a particular culture, and though people's movements among languages and cultures create very fuzzy lines between the two, our cultures and identities are still described and motivated by language. Furthermore, while we are not inextricably bound to any thought process rooted in the lexicon or grammar, our language does affect our worldview in important ways.[25] Thus, when children are encouraged to abandon the tongue of their grandparents and of their cultural heritage, the loss is deeper than mere words. Tony Johnson and Arlita Rhoan, both teachers of heritage languages in Oregon (Chinuk Wawa and Sahaptin, respectively), have argued that their languages are the key to the survival of their cultural identity and heritage.[26] Joshua Fishman, who has researched lesser-known languages for over fifty years, would concur, as he wrote:

> *Such a huge part of every ethnoculture is linguistically expressed that it is not wrong to say that most ethnocultural behaviours would be impossible without their expression via the particular language with which these behaviors have been traditionally associated ... every sociocultural collectivity*

> *interested in doing so has the right to strive for its own*
> *perceived authenticity via the language of its own preference.*[27]

The importance of heritage languages to Native Americans is great, and carries with it the knowledge and values of their ancestors. One Klamath language teacher stated:

> *Our kids may be plugged into their culture in three or four*
> *ways, but they can't be completely integrated into their culture*
> *until they learn the language. It fills in the gaps.*[28]

Many scholars have written about the strong link between language and culture. Stephen Greymorning of the Arapaho Nation in Wyoming, and professor of Anthropology and Native American Studies at the University of Montana, voiced the fear that language loss signals cultural loss as well:

> *I am really worried if we lose our language we won't be able*
> *to think in the Arapaho way. If we lose our language we will*
> *lose our ceremonies and ourselves because our life is our*
> *language, and it is our language that makes us strong.*[29]

Language and Identity

Modern philosophers argue that our identity is not a permanent "thing" that we are born with or acquire in our early years, but rather is in constant flux, created and recreated in our social dialogue with those around us. If the dialogues we enter into are radically different in our private and public spheres, they may painfully call into question who we are compared to who we are supposed to be.[30] Operating in two cultures, the home culture and the school culture, can be a confusing and frustrating experience for Native American students, who struggle to form a self-identity and a sense of belonging in two different cultural settings, one of which is not appreciated by the other. Western education has attempted to replace community structures with school structures, making it more difficult for Native American students to build a complete identity that incorporates who they are at home and who they are supposed to be at school.[31]

The gap between home and school dialogues can be bridged through heritage-language acquisition, giving students a chance to gain a deeper understanding of the cultural and value system from which they come, in comparison to those which they encounter at school. This understanding will assist them in navigating both systems, and will ultimately give them broader communicative abilities than their monolingual peers.[32]

Many people from Oregon's Native American communities have stressed the connection between their language and their identity as Oregon's indigenous peoples.[33] An important aspect of this identity is recognizing the uniqueness of each of Oregon's tribes; they cannot be conflated with each other or with tribes from other regions of the continent, as every tribe has its own history, traditions, and cultural norms. The myriad of languages spoken by Oregon's tribes testifies to their individuality and distinctness from other tribes. It also testifies to their nationhood and sovereignty.

Language and Sovereignty

Issues of sovereignty play largely into the inclusion of Oregon's Native languages in public schools. Many Native American tribes in the U.S. have treaties with the federal government recognizing them as sovereign nations. This means that they exist as nations within a nation, and as such, have special status that other minority groups do not have. The sovereignty is inherent, not given, as Native Americans were the original inhabitants of this region. Because their languages and cultures are also the original languages and cultures of this part of the world, they are protected by special laws (which will be discussed in the next section). This fact is especially important for their preservation, because unlike immigrant languages and cultures, these languages are based in this geographical region, and are spoken and practiced nowhere else in the world; if a Native American language ceases to be spoken here, it can not be retrieved anywhere else.

Myra Johnson emphasizes the importance of language to her tribe's sovereignty, and the fact that it represents their citizenship not only of the United States, but of the Warm Springs Nation.[34] Wendell Jim, the General Director of the Education Branch at the Confederated Tribes of Warm Springs, confirms her assertion, saying,

> *The survival of who we are as people, our heritage, our culture, sovereignty, everything that is tied to us being a unique people is related to the Native languages, our Indian languages.*

Retaining Oregon's Native languages is not only important for the sake of Oregon's tribes. The languages form a vital part of the state's cultural history and carry immense and invaluable knowledge about the region's geography, natural resources, and local art and music. Tony Johnson (of Grand Ronde) has emphasized that much of what people (Native Americans and settlers alike) needed to survive in this region was encoded in the languages spoken here.[35] In her speech on

March 8th, 2001, to the Oregon Senate's Education Committee in support of a bill that would help solidify the status of Oregon's Native languages in public classrooms, state Senator Kate Brown said:

> *American Indian languages of Oregon are vital and*
> *irreplaceable elements of our region's heritage and*
> *culture. They contribute to renewed cultural pride and self-*
> *determination for Native Oregonians. Languages contain*
> *generations of wisdom going back to antiquity. Our languages*
> *contain a significant part of the world's knowledge and*
> *wisdom ... I really think it's essential to all Oregonians, not*
> *just American Indians.*

As will be discussed in the next section, Native American languages are protected by special state and federal laws, most of which refer exclusively to public education, because they are the original tongues of federally recognized nations.

Policies that Affect Oregon's Native Language Programs

Several bills and measures have been passed at the state and federal levels to address the role and status of Native American languages in public education. Other documents have emerged from federal committees on education recommending that Native American cultural and linguistic material be included in public curricula in order to ensure that all students have equal opportunity to succeed in school. As discussed earlier, much educational policy depends on national political trends and public values. Wendell Jim and Myra Johnson, both of whom have been very active in the creation of legislation to support Native American language-revitalization efforts, remarked that their success depended not so much on how they worded their legislation, but on rising national movements to recognize and incorporate Native American languages into educational programs.

The laws discussed here have great potential to aid in the revitalization efforts of Native American languages. However, as Larry Cuban, Professor of Education at Stanford University, points out, classroom practices often do not match political policies. Administrators and teachers may ignore directives because they lack funds or time, or because the policies aren't viable in actual practice. Cuban compares the relationship between policy and practice to the relationship between the surface and depths of the sea; great storms may rage at the surface (policy) level, while not a grain of sand is stirred at the ocean bottom (classroom).[36] Therefore, the efficacy of federal and state education policy as it pertains to Native American students rests in the hands of educators and their administrators; their knowledge about language policy and willingness to implement it are essential elements in the revitalization process.

In this section, some of the most prominent policies that affect the incorporation of linguistic and cultural materials in public schools in the state of Oregon and across the United States will be outlined. The section begins with the Native American Languages Act, the first federal policy to directly support Native American languages in the United States, and then explores other activities at the national level and the state level. Finally, charter school legislation is discussed, a movement that has appeared at both the federal and state levels, and may be of positive use for tribes struggling to implement effective language programs in their districts' public schools.

Federal Level Policies

Native American Languages Act (1990)

The Native American Languages Act (NALA) marked a complete change from previous U.S. laws and policies that had ignored, downplayed, obstructed, or otherwise acted to eradicate Native American languages. By this monumental act, Congress gave special status to Native American languages, recognizing their importance to the cultures they encode and to the nation in general. The Act states that it is in the best interest of the United States for all of its citizens to achieve their full potential, and that academic achievement and performance are directly tied to respect for and support of a child's heritage language. The Act thus forbids the restriction of public use of Native American languages, including use in public school classrooms. Furthermore, it permits exceptions to teacher certification requirements for teachers of Native American languages, if such requirements hinder their ability to teach in programs funded by the federal government. It also encourages the use of Native American languages as the medium of instruction in public schools. In the realm of higher education, it encourages institutions to grant foreign-language credits to those students who speak or have had instruction in a Native American language.

Wendell Jim was one of the people who testified in favor of the NALA. In general, he was pleased to see Congress take action in favor of the nation's original languages, but was disappointed that no funds were appropriated to support the kinds of programs it suggests are important. However, in 1992 the Act was revised to include an annual grant of $2 million for Native American language programs. While this is a start, it is not enough to support language programs for the 561 federally recognized tribes in the United States.[37] Though the funding is not sufficient, the Act does promise to facilitate language programs by ensuring that federal education and language policies do not restrict their existence.

According to Jim, the most important aspect of the NALA was the education that took place as tribes shared their experiences and testimonies with lawmakers:

> *I believe the lawmakers knew some of the impacts, or had some knowledge of what had occurred [to the languages], but when the tribes testified, the tribal people spoke from their own perspectives of the impact, and I think it really opened the lawmakers' eyes to [how important it was] to recognize Native Americans and their contributions.*

Report of the Indian Nations at Risk Task Force (1991)

In 1991, soon after the passage of the NALA, the U.S. Secretary of Education convened the Indian Nations at Risk Task Force, which explored issues surrounding the failure of the United States public school system to adequately educate its American Indian and Alaska Native students. The Task Force released a report that states several National Education Goals, one of which is to "maintain Native languages and cultures."[38] The report also includes the Indian Student Bill of Rights, listing various facets of education that Native American students have a right to. One of these rights is the right to an appropriately tailored linguistic and cultural environment. Overall, the report reaffirms the importance of Native American languages to the nation and to the educational system, with specific recommendations to support these languages in schools.

The report cites Native American dropout rates, which are the highest in the nation, and students' negative attitudes about school to demonstrate that Native American students are at risk in the public school system. It indicates that this is partially a result of historical and continued attacks on their heritage languages and cultures, as well as an unfriendly school environment that presents only a Western perspective of school subjects. Finally, it states that it is the responsibility of the United States government to provide enriching linguistic and cultural school curricula, seek the knowledge and involvement of parents and elders in doing so, and address the overt and subtle racism that Native American students face in school.

In addition to predicting a better general attitude about school among Native American students if their languages are presented in the school setting, the report refers to the intellectual, cognitive, and social benefits of heritage-language acquisition. It describes specific school programs that have shown significant student achievement increases through the use of Native American languages and cultural curricula. The report strongly supports the use of culturally appropriate curricula, stating, "Schools that respect and support a student's language and culture are significantly more successful in educating those children."[39] However, the Task Force's recommendations are not limited to Native American students: it recommends that school officials and educators give a multicultural focus to the curriculum of the entire school, and encourages local and state governments to allocate funds for these changes.

Comprehensive Federal Indian Education Policy Statement (March 1997)

The Comprehensive Federal Indian Education Policy Statement was submitted to the White House by tribal leaders and Indian educators, with assistance from the National Congress of American Indians, the National Indian Education Association, the Native American Rights Fund, and the National Advisory Council on Indian Education. The statement calls for the federal government to take several steps to improve educational opportunities for Native American students, including incorporating Native American languages into public classrooms. It asks the federal government to provide monetary and technical support for Native American language and cultural material, and to encourage non-tribal institutions serving Native American students to recognize and include Native American language and culture instruction upon tribal request.

Notably, the statement also emphasizes the importance of consulting with tribal leaders and educators before implementing any policies, rules, actions, or decisions that affect Native American education. It calls for the government to support tribal education laws, and recognizes Native American inherent tribal sovereignty and unique government-to-government relations, as well as the special status of Native American languages and cultures in the United States. By doing so, it reaffirms Native American sovereignty, and recognizes that Native American communities have the knowledge and ability to meet their children's educational needs.

No Child Left Behind Act - Title VII: Indian, Native Hawaiian, and Alaska Native Education (2002)

Title VII of the No Child Left Behind Act (NCLB), which was introduced by the Bush administration in 2001 and signed into law on January 8th, 2002, recognizes the "unique educational and culturally related academic needs of [Indian children]," and provides funding for programs that address these needs. It makes funds available for "culturally related activities" to supplement (not replace) standard programs for Native American students. These special programs must show academic benefits for Native American children and must show that the students' culturally (and linguistically) related academic needs are met. It also encourages "activities that ... incorporate appropriately qualified tribal elders and seniors." The Act makes grants available for special programs and projects for the education of Native American youth, including bilingual and bicultural programs and projects. It also provides money for educational research benefiting Native American students, as well as for training Native American teachers.

Unfortunately, though Native American "language needs" are mentioned in the NCLB Act, and bilingual curricular projects are supported, very little attention is given to the role of heritage-language instruction in public schools. Indeed, the only specific references to Native American language instruction are made for "special needs" children who perform either above or below their average classmates. Section 7134 of Title VII encourages "meeting the educational needs of ... gifted and talented children ... [by] demonstrating and exploring the use of Indian languages and exposure to Indian cultural traditions." The following section provides grants to "coordinate the provision of any needed special services for conditions such as disabilities and English language skill deficiencies." Thus, heritage languages are treated as special subjects for gifted students to dabble in, or as obstacles in the way of learning for students with low achievement. They are not, however, recognized as important elements of learning for all Native American students. This is true only of the continental United States; special provisions are made for Alaska Natives and Hawaiian Natives supporting the use of Native languages for purposes of instruction, and for the protection and continued use of their languages.

Esther Martinez Native Languages Preservation Act (2006)

The most recent federal legislation pertaining to Native American languages was named after a Tewa storyteller and linguist who was killed in an auto accident, and is much more supportive of Native American languages than the NCLB Act. It is an amendment to the Native American Programs Act of 1974, which was an act of very broad scope providing a variety of grants and services to Native Americans. Under the new Act, grants can be made to Native American tribes for language-revitalization purposes, including language immersion programs and language classes. Under these grants, five hundred hours of instruction must be provided per year to a minimum of ten children in immersion (under the age of seven) or fifteen children in language classes, with the ultimate goal of fluency. This act therefore recognizes the dire situation that many Native American languages are in, and takes an important step in providing economic support for their revitalization. It also funds the types of programs that have the most potential to produce proficient speakers. Methods of teaching for language proficiency will be discussed in more detail in Chapter Five.

State Level Policies

In Oregon, state-level legislation has also provided support for Native American language programs. These education policies have had both cultural and linguistic components, and demonstrate that the state of Oregon is concerned about preserving its valuable linguistic resources. The first of these bills, Senate Bill 103, did not specifically mention Native Americans or their languages, but provided opportunities for schools to incorporate culturally and linguistically appropriate lessons into their curricula. Subsequent legislation pertained directly to Native American languages, and paved the way for Oregon districts to fully integrate language programs into their schools.

Oregon Senate Bill 103 (1999)

Senate Bill 103 directs the Oregon Department of Education to evaluate the types of diversity present in Oregon's public schools, and based on this evaluation, to increase efforts to identify and integrate successful curricula for multicultural education programs. It directs the Superintendent of Public Instruction to seek funding to develop and implement materials aimed at multicultural student populations in individual districts, depending on their demographics. For districts with large numbers of Native American students, this may mean incorporating tribal histories and cultural traditions into History, Social Studies, Music, and Art classes, or even supporting Native American language courses in the public schools.

Oregon Senate Bill 690 (2001)

Following closely on the heels of the more general Senate Bill 103, Senate Bill 690 gives specific attention to the linguistic needs of Native Americans. This bill, which took effect in January 2002, allows speakers of Oregon's Native languages to obtain special certificates which permit them to teach in public school classrooms. Each tribe in Oregon establishes its own criteria by which to assess the language skills of these teachers. There are several provisions in the Bill stipulating that unless the Native American language teachers also have a state-issued teaching certificate, they can only teach the language for which they have obtained a special license, and only in a classroom with a state-certified teacher present. Language teachers must also attend a "technical assistance program," in which a licensed teacher with three or more years of teaching experience assists the language teacher with curriculum development, classroom management, and other skills learned in state-approved teaching programs.[40]

The bill was introduced by the Confederated Tribes of Warm Springs, and spearheaded by Myra Johnson, the director of the language program there. She had heard of similar legislation in other states, and asked the tribal lobbyist to formulate a law for presentation before the Oregon legislature. "It was really overwhelming to know that we were going to possibly make a difference in the state of Oregon by legislation in regards to our Native languages. So it was really exciting," she said of the experience. However, she refuses to take personal credit for the success of the bill, attributing it instead to a general trend of support for Native American languages across the nation:

> *I don't credit it with just myself. I think that it was something that was happening across the nation: Native language programs being recognized, as well as the importance of Native languages to the people. It was actually coming forth across the nation, and I felt like it was just a really ideal time for that to happen in the state of Oregon.*

Johnson says that elders and teachers from all the tribes in Oregon gave testimony at the state capitol in Salem three times, impressing on legislators the seriously endangered condition of the languages, and the extreme value of the cultural traditions carried by each one. Tribal members gave testimonies in many of Oregon's indigenous languages, including Sahaptin, Northern Paiute, Wasco, Chinuk Wawa, and Walla Walla. These testimonies asserted again and again that it is only tribal members who are able to determine teacher readiness and classroom standards for Oregon's Native languages, as only they can fluently speak and understand these languages.

Senate Bill 690 has been a major victory for teachers of Native Oregon languages, because it means that people who are fluent speakers, but who do not have the time, money, and/or inclination to attend a four-year degree program to obtain their teaching license can still impart their knowledge to their tribe's children within the public education system. It also recognizes the importance of Oregon's indigenous languages, both to the state and to Oregon's Native American children, stating, "The Legislative Assembly declares that teaching American Indian languages is essential to the proper education of American Indian children." This is a far cry from policies at the turn of the twentieth century regarding the education of Native American children, and a welcome one.

However, the bill is not perfect, and has not guaranteed Native American languages a place in the public schools where Native American children are taught. In many of Oregon's schools, other subjects take precedence over Native American languages, and so no room is made in the daily schedule for the newly licensed language teachers to teach their subjects. Not viewing them as "real" teachers, some administrators don't include Native American language teachers in teacher planning meetings and trainings. The result is that the language teachers aren't as informed as other teachers about the school and students. And more than one tribe has reported difficulty with acquiring a physical space in which to teach in the schools.[41]

Peggy McIntosh, the Associate Director of the Wellesley College Center for Research on Women, faced similar problems when attempting to add literature by female authors to a college reading list.[42] While the other educators agreed that literature by women was very valuable, they refused to make room for it by removing any literature by men. In the case of Native American languages, administrators may acknowledge the value of teaching them in the classroom, but are resistant to incorporating them at the perceived expense of other subjects and classroom space.

Oregon American Indian/Alaska Native Education State Plan (Revised, 2002)

The Oregon American Indian/Alaska Native Education State Plan outlines the specific goals and strategies of the Oregon Department of Education in serving the educational needs of American Indian and Alaska Native students in the state of Oregon. It recognizes the unacceptably high dropout rate and general underachievement of Native American students, and seeks to rectify the situation through the implementation of a strategy that supports the specific educational needs of Native American youth and adults. Among other things, the plan commits strongly to incorporating Native American cultural, historical, and linguistic materials in public education settings, recognizing that Native American students will achieve better academically if they feel that their heritage is respected in the public school system. The plan also encourages individual school districts to implement curricula specifically designed to meet the needs of its Native American students.

Charter Schools

Despite policies that support Native American language instruction and the incorporation of cultural curricula in public schools, many of Oregon's Native American language teachers and administrators feel that their local school districts have been unresponsive to their needs. The policies discussed so far provide little or no funding, and while they encourage the inclusion of appropriate linguistic and cultural material, they do not mandate it. What actually happens in Oregon's classrooms depends on policy implementation by administrators and teachers, and whether it is because they are unaware of the benefits of incorporating Native American linguistic and cultural curricula, or because (more than likely) they lack the funds and time required to do so, Native American languages are being marginalized or even excluded from public schools.[43]

Another option that some tribes are turning to, therefore, is that of creating their own school. The federal government provides special provisions for public schools with flexible structures, rules, and activities called charter schools. These schools encourage innovative teaching methods, but still require rigorous assessment of student progress, and are not exempt from statewide achievement tests.[44] Title V of the No Child Left Behind Act supports charter schools with funds and grants, and aims to increase the number of charter schools throughout the nation by encouraging individual states to get behind the movement. The state of Oregon has charter school legislation called ORS Chapter 338, which was passed in 1999 and establishes charters as subsidiaries of their local school district. They may exist as separate programs within an existing school, originate from a pre-existing public school, or start completely new.[45] Both the Confederated Tribes of Siletz Indians and the Confederated Tribes of the Umatilla Indian Reservation have taken advantage of this legislation and have created charter high schools: the Siletz Valley Early College Academy and Nixyaawii. At Nixyaawii, students can choose between taking Umatilla, Walla Walla, or Nez Perce/Cayuse. In 2006 Nixyaawii was chosen Oregon Charter School of the Year and that fall, Native American languages were incorporated into the football awards ceremony.

Wendell Jim of Warm Springs has been especially positive about charters, stating,

> *Charter schools gave the tribes the flexibility to develop language programs, to be innovative, and to implement our traditional oral histories and oral ways of learning and teaching the languages.*

One way in which charter school legislation facilitates Native American language revitalization is by allowing up to one half of the school's full-time teachers to teach without licenses. They must register through the Teacher Standards and Practices Commission, but are not required to hold specific degrees or licenses.[46] As discussed in the preceding section about Senate Bill 690, many fluent speakers of Oregon's Native languages are too old to consider pursuing a four-year degree and teaching license. Younger teachers may not have the time or money to do so, or may live too far away from an institution of higher education to consider the option practically. Many of them are simultaneously improving their skills in the language by working with elders while teaching the language to others. This makes it impractical to pursue studies far away. Allowing non-licensed language speakers to teach gets more teachers into the classrooms faster, in a situation where time is of the essence.

Charter schools remain one option for Oregon tribes to incorporate Native American languages and cultural material in classrooms when their programs face exclusion in regular schools. However, starting a charter school is a complicated process, and requires much time, planning, and funding. As a result, most tribes continue to seek their place within the traditional public school rubric, where they face escalating challenges due to funding cuts and mandated academic programs. Furthermore, schools have political motivations to stick to English instruction, and as we discussed earlier, political factors are often much stronger than pedagogical research in determining school policy. Native American language programs are encountering increased obstacles from the revival of English-only movements that have garnered support in many parts of the United States.

English-Only Legislation and Native American Languages

Recall from Chapter One that the exclusive use of English was used as a tool to eradicate Native American languages and to assimilate this region's First Peoples to the new nation's value system. Similar efforts were used to assimilate recent immigrants to the dominant culture, and this goal continues to spur political pressure to ban the use of any language but English in public schools. California and Arizona have both recently passed English-only laws pertaining to education within their respective states. California's Proposition 227, adopted by voters in 1998, requires that English be the language of instruction in all California public classrooms, including English as a Second Language (ESL) classrooms.

Throughout the 1920s, there were strong English-only movements in various states, many of which supported the teaching of English as a means of spawning patriotism. A more insidious reason was the notion that English was an inherently better language than others, allowing clearer and more logical thought processes. It was thus considered essential to the continuation of a functioning democracy.[47] Furthermore, children were thought to be handicapped by bilingualism, and general pedagogical opinion at the beginning of the twentieth century warned of the dangers of being bilingual for children's mental development.[48] Linguists and educators have since recognized that no language is inherently better than another. Every language is capable of developing what it needs. They also point to the improved abstract cognitive abilities of children who speak more than one language. However, economic and political factors have shaped English-only campaigns far more than academic research has, and they have continued to gain ground in many states.

In the 1980s, English-only movements became popular because people feared that non-English speakers would depress wages and take their jobs. They also feared that bilingual education using heritage languages as the mode of instruction would create situations of "societal bilingualism" and "ethnic separatism," and they linked bilingualism with ethnic splintering.[49] Nationalistic trends in recent years have further supported English-only movements, and there is general public opposition to funding non-English language instruction in public schools.[50]

However, it should be noted that a great number of multilingual societies worldwide have existed quite peacefully. Before white settlement on this continent, it was common in many tribes for people to be multilingual and communicate, trade, and intermarry with people of different tribes. Present-day Switzerland provides another example, with four official languages spoken within its national borders. Indeed, the ethnic splintering that people fear can be traced to more deeply rooted social inequalities. Baron states, "Generally speaking, linguistic friction and violence occur around the globe not where language rights are protected, but where they have been suppressed."[51] Indeed, language minorities may regard English-only legislation as an affront to their individuality and an attempt to exclude them from mainstream society, leading to further divisiveness.[52]

English-only movements pose dangers to Native American language-revitalization efforts because they may block language teaching in public schools. It is hard to predict how any particular piece of English-only legislation would affect language programs, but Native American language teachers and administrators fear that such legislation will hinder their programs at best and eliminate them entirely at worst. Wendell Jim believes that Native American languages may be protected in the first round of English-only legislation, but as people grow more and more accustomed to the idea, support for Native language instruction will shrink, until they are eliminated entirely from public schools.

The arguments for heritage-language education should in no way be seen as a call to abandon English-language instruction. Most parents (Native American and immigrant parents included) in the United States recognize the economic and social benefits of having a firm command of Standard English, and want their children to speak it.[53] However, we haven't seen the English-only movement bring attention to more and better ways of teaching English. We have only seen it attempting to deprive other languages of attention and funding. This leads us to conclude that the English-only movement is politically rather than pedagogically motivated, and is acting as a disguise for more deeply rooted fears and discriminatory notions.

Indeed, the English language has no need for legal protection. It is spoken by more than 97 percent of the people in the United States, it is the dominant language in Australia, the British Isles, Canada, New Zealand, and numerous former British colonies, and it is the largest second language learned globally. In fact, more people learn English as a second (or third or fourth) language than there are native speakers of the language. This is the case despite no federal sanctioning of English as the official language of the United States.[54] The economic and social status of English are effective safeguards against its demise, and as long as it is a language of economic and social prestige, people will learn it and use it, even to the neglect of their own heritage languages. While English remains in a very safe position worldwide, we are in grave danger of losing the many original languages of our state and nation.

English-Plus Legislation

Though English-only movements are widespread and appear to be gaining prominence in many regions of the United States, they face positive resistance. Many states, including Oregon, Rhode Island, Washington, and New Mexico, along with some major cities, have passed English-plus resolutions, which support people's rights to master both English and another language.[55] Oregon's Senate Joint Resolution 16, passed in 1989, states that English is already very prominent in the state, obviating official-English legislation, and concludes that "[the] use of diverse languages in business, government and private affairs, and the presence of diverse cultures is welcomed, encouraged, and protected in Oregon."

At the national level, Representative Jose E. Serrano (D-NY) introduced English-plus legislation in January 2005 at the 109th Session of Congress. The bill, entitled "English Plus Resolution" (H. Con. Res. 9), specifically stated the importance of English to the nation, but also recognized the need to "conserve and develop" other languages spoken by citizens of the United States. It stated that not only is widespread multilingualism a tremendous national resource that puts us at an advantage in the global market, it also aids us in national security, and helps diffuse cross-cultural misunderstandings. The bill also refers to Native American languages, resolving to assist tribes in the preservation of their languages. Unfortunately, the bill was referred to the Subcommittee on Education Reform and never made it to the House floor. While some states have been able to pass similar resolutions, the present national political climate does not encourage the support of non-English languages, including the national treasures that are the indigenous languages of the United States.

Conclusion

Introducing Native American languages back into public school classrooms would help Native American student achievement. It would serve as a means of reaffirming their identities, boosting their self-esteem, and demonstrating that the schools care about their heritage and communities. It would also potentially improve their cognitive and metalinguistic skills. Such results have been predicted by Native American elders and teachers, affirmed by research, and supported by several laws and acts. However, obstacles remain, not the least of which is possible English-only legislation in the state of Oregon. Other obstacles include lack of funding for legislation and lack of support at the district and school level.

It is clear from dropout and achievement test statistics that the U.S. education system has historically failed Native American students. To reverse this trend, what is needed is the recognition, not only by the government, but also by individual districts and schools, of the importance of Oregon's heritage languages and cultures to all Oregonians. These languages encode the historical and still-unique cultures of the region, but are spoken almost exclusively by a limited number of older speakers. While providing instruction or using these languages as the language of instruction in Oregon schools could never rectify the wrongs done in the past, it would be one step in preventing further wrongs in the future as the United States assists in revitalizing what it once actively sought to destroy.

Chapter Four

The History and Context of Oregon Tribal Language Archival Collections

David G. Lewis (*Confederated Tribes of Grand Ronde*) *and* **Deanna Kingston** (*King Island Inupiaq*)

> *"[C]onsidering the interest which every nation has in extending and strengthening the authority of reason and justice among the people around them, it would be useful to acquire what knowledge you can of the state of morality, religion and information among them, as it may better enable those who endeavor to civilize and instruct them, to adapt their measures to the existing nations and practices of those on whom they are to operate." Thomas Jefferson's instructions to Lewis and Clark*[1]

> *"Records [of Native American peoples of Oregon] have been scattered, records have been burned, records have been lost." Naomi Riebe (Upper Umpqua Indian Council)*[2]

Introduction

In this chapter, we focus on the archival collections of Oregon Native American language materials and the historical context of their creation. It is due to this history that many of these collections are not located in the state of Oregon, and it is only through the efforts of dedicated tribal members and staff that Oregon tribes have copies of such records. First, we discuss the history of Western scholarship of Oregon Native American languages, and how these collections privileged Western scholars over the Native American communities from whom the languages originated. This is followed by critiques of these archival collections by Native American scholars, followed by reasons why these materials should be used in Oregon Native American language revitalization efforts. We then give a brief overview of the societal context behind the creation of these collections in order to understand the issues that should be considered prior to using them.

We finish by giving examples of where these materials are so that readers may more easily locate them.

History, Privilege, Action

Archival collections of language materials are the primary source materials for contemporary studies in linguistics and for the preservation and restoration of traditional languages by Native American tribes. For many tribes, these primary source materials exist in widely scattered archival collections in universities, museums, and ethnological society repositories. Many of these collections were created at the same time that the fields of anthropology and linguistics were being developed in the United States, and as such, must be considered products of the thinking of that time. In other words, understanding as much of the mindset of the collectors as possible will allow tribes to gain insight into what information was recorded at the time and why.

In the late nineteenth and early twentieth centuries, anthropologists and linguists created significant archival and artifact collections about Oregon Native American cultures. Their efforts were driven, in part, by two related assumptions held by members of colonizing nations. The first assumption was based upon the idea of "cultural evolution" or "social Darwinism." As it implies, this idea was related to Darwin's evolutionary theory, but applied to societies and cultures. Under this theoretical framework, popular from the 1870s to the early twentieth century and exemplified by Lewis Henry Morgan's *Ancient Society*, social scientists sought to understand their societies' own distant past by looking at so-called "primitive peoples." This theory stated that all human societies evolve from a savage state, through barbarianism, to civilization. Morgan, in particular, outlined the characteristics of the different stages. For instance, when looking at economic systems, he assigned the classification of "savage" to those peoples who foraged (hunted, gathered, and fished) their food from their local environment. Barbarian peoples were those doing simple agricultural practices, such as "slash-and-burn" agriculture. Civilized peoples were those who had developed an intensive agricultural system that incorporated irrigation and fertilization strategies for growing their crops and had developed industry.[3] This idea—that white society was more civilized than Native American societies—can be seen not only in the writings of whites, but in those of nineteenth-century Native Americans. For instance, one female seminary student at the Cherokee Female Seminary, wrote "O! that all, especially among the Cherokees could but learn the vast importance of a good education.

This and this only will place us on equality with other enlightened and cultivated nations."[4] By researching contemporary hunters/gatherers (i.e., "savages"), early social scientists thought they would gain insights into their own past, so they recorded language, kinship practices, food-procurement strategies, religions and rituals, etc., of these foraging peoples. In other words, these aspects of indigenous peoples' cultures became data for social scientific theories about how cultures evolved.

At the same time that these ideas were prevalent, the scientific method became a prominent practice in colonizing societies. Under the Western scientific paradigm, a researcher must collect as many data points as possible in order to make generalizations. So, to understand monarch butterflies, researchers would not just take one monarch butterfly to study, but would get many examples in order to know that their generalizations are applicable to all cases of monarch butterflies. In order to understand the diversity and nature of human cultures and languages, American anthropologists and linguists in the late nineteenth and early twentieth centuries turned to those peoples living within U.S. territory. Many notable American anthropologists and linguists got their start in Oregon, which helped crystallize the anthropology and linguistic disciplines. However, when social scientists began collecting data, they found indigenous peoples continuing to die at an alarming rate due to introduced diseases, the final Indian wars, and acts of genocide. Death rates reached as high as 75-95 percent in some Native American communities. Thus, nineteenth-century social scientists became concerned that "their" "data," in the form of indigenous peoples' cultures, would disappear before they could record them.

Rather than raising an alarm, the fact that peoples were dying at very high rates was seen as proof of natural selection (Social Darwinism at work) in which more savage, primitive peoples died while more advanced colonial peoples survived. These high death rates contributed to the second assumption that drove the creation of archival materials, which is that Indians were a "vanishing race." In order to capture the data held in indigenous cultures before they disappeared to science, Western scholars entered into a kind of collecting frenzy, gathering as much about Native American cultures as possible, including artifacts, human remains, and linguistic data.[5] This became known as "salvage ethnography," which had a corresponding form in linguistics called "salvage linguistics."[6] Folklorists as well wanted to assure they could continue to practice their discipline after the tribes went extinct.[7]

Although the early recording of languages was done to enable communication (e.g., there are numerous Chinook Jargon dictionaries created for this purpose) and to convert Native American peoples to Christianity, the academic research was done in the salvage mode. Thus, significant collections of Native American intellectual knowledge were created in order to save cultural and linguistic data, propagating the notion that Native American people are only objects of scientific inquiry rather than important actors in their own right. Subsequently, the access to and use of these collections came to be limited to scholars, in order to advance scientific understandings.[8] What is interesting is that scholars found that Native American languages were as complex as English and other European languages, which compelled linguists to break with the evolutionary model in the realm of language.[9]

It would be difficult to point out a comprehensive collection of Oregon Native American language archival materials; in fact, there are no primary linguistic archival collections in Oregon outside of tribal communities (with one exception, to be discussed later). These materials are archived in repositories that are related to the work and careers of some of the earliest anthropologists and linguists in the United States. And since these scholars usually operated out of institutions on the East Coast, their papers and fieldnotes often reside in those places today.

These early anthropologists and linguists established the foundations of anthropology and linguistics in the United States. The most influential of these early anthropologists, Franz Boas, known as "the father of American anthropology," worked on many tribal cultures throughout the Pacific Northwest. In Oregon, Boas personally researched the Chinookan languages, including Upper and Lower Chinook, Clackamas, and also Tillamook and Chinook Jargon. Following his appointment as the Director of the Smithsonian Institution's Bureau of American Ethnology, Boas sent many of his students to Oregon, many to the Grand Ronde and Siletz reservations, to complete his work on the Chinookan languages, and to research the many other Native American languages from western Oregon. In his various capacities, Boas directed Jaime de Angulo, James Owen Dorsey, Leo J. Frachtenberg, Melville Jacobs, May Mandelbaum, Archie Phinney, Edward Sapir, and Leslie Spier, all of whom worked on Oregon Native languages.

These students of Boas became some of the most prominent social scientists of the nineteenth and twentieth centuries and later established careers at some of the oldest and most renowned universities in the United States. Franz Boas himself worked at Columbia University, Edward Sapir at Yale University, Albert Kroeber and T. T. Waterman at the University of California, Berkeley, and Melville Jacobs and James Owen Dorsey at the University of Washington. All of these scholars were members of anthropological and linguistic associations, and most conducted work for the Bureau of American Ethnology (BAE) (now a part of the Smithsonian Institution, which houses the BAE's records in the National Anthropological Archives). Others were employed at museums, like the Field Museum in Chicago.

The Oregon Native American language collections are archived in institutions most closely associated to the researchers that worked at them. A majority are in the National Anthropological Archives in Suitland, Maryland, which contains the collections from the BAE. The University of Washington has vast collections related to the research of Melville and Elizabeth Jacobs and many of their research associates. In addition, the Bancroft Library at the University of California, Berkeley, holds collections created from the research of Alfred Kroeber and his associates. Theodore Stern's records are located at the University of Oregon and have only recently become accessible to researchers following his death in 2005. Stern worked extensively on Umatilla and Klamath culture and language. David and Kathryn French at Reed College worked extensively with Walter Dyk and Dell Hymes. Their combined work on the Warm Springs languages is in the Walter Dyk Collection at the American Philosophical Society in Philadelphia. Several other institutions hold collections from individual scholars, including Columbia University, Yale University, and the University of Chicago. (See Appendix One for listing of these various archives. Please note that this list is not exhaustive and is only meant to start interested parties in their search.)

Contemporary researchers must travel to these archival repositories to gain access to primary resource materials. To do this requires an investment of time and money. Often, when tribal members arrive at these archival repositories, they find that usage is restricted, or that the archivists will not allow them access to the materials they are interested in because of their fragile condition. For instance, the University of Washington imposed a research application procedure on the Melville and Elizabeth Jacobs collections, creating a layer of bureaucracy that did not exist for many other collections. This application layer was removed in 2006. In an additional example, in order to use the research room at the National Anthropological

Archives, a researcher must have a sponsor from the Smithsonian Institution. In short, the impediments to Native American people seeking out critical parts of their language for restoration and preservation are daunting.

For indigenous peoples working to restore their languages, limited access to these collections is clearly a problem. From the worldwide indigenous critique of imperialism and colonization, a critical analysis of archives and museums as centers of imperial power has emerged. Archives and museums concentrate indigenous intellectual knowledge and then control it by determining access policies, deciding who is allowed to use the collections, and by valuing the opinions of non-indigenous scholars over tribal language speakers with less formal education. And, since the archival centers are usually far removed from the indigenous territories and lands and indigenous people have few opportunities or resources to travel to them, they have less overall access to the collections. Thus, in order to locate and use these collections and to obtain funding for language revitalization, it is imperative that indigenous people gain access to the systems of education that will give them the tools that will allow them to study and work on their languages.

In addition, each institution has different copyright policies with regard to the collections they hold. In general, once a collection has been accessioned in an archive, the person who donated it usually gives up any rights that he or she may have to the material and allows the institution to hold the copyright. This includes any materials on Native American cultures and languages gathered by scholars in the past. However, Native Americans claim, and many scholars agree, that this information is the intellectual and cultural property of the people who shared the knowledge with the scholar.[10] With this recognition of Native American intellectual property rights, many archival institutions are entering into different kinds of agreements with the tribes, agreements in which Native American rights to the knowledge are acknowledged.

There are distinctions between tribal collections and the collections created by anthropologists and linguists. The first distinction is in the intent of the collectors. For tribes, the intent is to preserve and restore their traditional language and for anthropologists and linguists, the intent is generally to collect data and store them for the good of humanity. A good example of a tribal collection is the Southwest Oregon Research Project sponsored by the Coquille Tribe and undertaken by University of Oregon graduate students. The students, many of whom were from Oregon tribes, copied thousands of pages of archival documents related to the tribal peoples of southwestern Oregon and participated in a process to give them (back) to all of the tribes in Oregon.

These reasons have at times worked alongside one another. However, critiques by tribal nations and Native American scholars question the intent of anthropologists, which is often to further their own careers rather than to help the tribes.[11] A collection created by a scholar may include more information on the technical aspects of the language, such as aspects of the grammar, whereas a tribal collection will have more information related to how the language is used and under what circumstances. A second distinction is that Native American tribes in Oregon only began their collections in the last thirty years and thus they may not be as extensive or as organized as those that were created over a hundred years ago.

Native American Critiques of Archival and Museum Collections

As has been pointed out by many scholars, archival and museum collections are the result of the colonization of North America by Europeans, and some Native Americans feel that they should be avoided for that very reason. Critical researchers such as Vine Deloria Jr. and Linda T. Smith point out that social scientists have operated within particular social, political, and economic contexts that have furthered their academic careers at the same time that Native American peoples, and their cultures and languages, have disappeared.[12] In other words, scholars often published the results of their research with little regard for the viability of the cultures and languages that they studied. This essentially privileges the work and lives of academic researchers over those of Native American people and tribes. Scientists have continued to operate within this privileged context through analyzing and publishing the information collected, thereby becoming the "public" experts on Native American culture. In addition, these scholarly writings have done little to help Native American communities preserve their languages. Hundreds of Native American languages are now extinct, with no known living speakers.

For tribal peoples, the work of outside scholars removes from the traditional culture bearers their rights to present their own perspectives on their culture and language, because the scholars are the recognized experts, not the people themselves.[13] For instance, in one extreme example in Southeastern Alaska, the anthropologist was called to the witness stand to testify about traditional Tlingit subsistence areas, while his primary informant, a Tlingit elder, sat in the courtroom and listened. The court gave more weight to the anthropologist's testimony.[14] This situation disempowers Native American people and tribes, politically, socially, and economically, in their ability to tell their own stories about their society from their point of view. Their perspectives are marginalized in favor of those of social scientists.

We can see the privileging of Western scholars over Native American tribal members through the actions of the United States federal government, which bases much of its information and policies about Native American peoples and tribal governments on the opinions of anthropologists.[15] In addition, the scholars' efforts have created a system of self-replication, where their protégés continue in their "school of thought," feeding the system that raises the researchers to a privileged status, higher than that of the Native American peoples of their research. As anthropologist Bea Medicine has pointed out, the system has worked so well that many Native American people now turn to the anthropological and linguistic texts to learn or re-learn their cultural heritage.[16] This phenomenon has been noticed by researchers, who now critique contemporary Native American societies, most recently the Chumash, for supposedly "inventing" their culture out of anthropology books.[17] Critiques in this vein publicly disempower Native American people struggling to maintain cultural and ancestral ties, which are necessary in the implementation of federal cultural-resource management laws (e.g., the Native American Graves Protection and Repatriation Act 1990 and the National Historic Preservation Act 1966).

In response to these critiques, many tribes maintain that their elder native language speakers are the true archival repositories and that anthropologically inspired collections and their resultant theories are fictional creations that should not be used. This perspective asserts that cultural knowledge never left the tribal communities and that what is really needed is for Native American people to focus their efforts within their communities and separate themselves from those records created by anthropologists and linguists. This is a valid argument for many tribes with an intact cultural core. However, the single greatest overriding factor that argues for using these archival collections in Oregon is that many Oregon Native American languages only survive in manuscript form, collected years ago by early anthropologists and linguists. Because of this, most Oregon tribes use textual sources along with information from their elder culture bearers. In addition, these archival collections can be useful, if not for the information itself, then for the understanding they can give contemporary tribal members of the historical relationships between Native Americans and Western scholars. Finally, as Native American archivist and librarian Cheryl Metoyer stated at a meeting in October 2004 of the Oregon Collaborative Project in Pendleton, Oregon, accessing and using the information recorded by these Western scholars stops the "uglification" of colonization because Native American tribes are using the information to further their own agendas and not those of Western scholars.

We also want to point out that these ethnographic archival collections would not have been possible without the contributions of the Oregon Native American tribal members who spoke the languages and chose to take part in the research. From the perspective of Native American communities, they too contributed to the creation of these archives by providing skilled research informants who were willing to work with the researchers from another culture, often under trying circumstances. Their efforts should not be in vain. The contributions of these Native American informants are largely overlooked by historical studies of anthropology or linguistics, where the careers of the academic researchers take precedence. We wish to counteract this tendency and highlight some of these early Native American collaborators below. The information these individuals provided helped create various academic disciplines in the United States, which contribute to our current understandings of American Indian cultures, societies, and languages.

Fortunately, the Native American critique of anthropology has had a positive effect on the field. Anthropologists in growing numbers have created new research processes in which tribal members take an active role in the research, and in which the decision-making power is shared equally between Native American tribal members and scholars. In some instances, scholars have specifically asked Native American tribes to dictate the research agenda and are now acknowledging tribal intellectual property rights. The changes can be seen in the proliferation of new and alternative anthropology sub-fields such as ethnohistory, applied anthropology, critical anthropology, public anthropology, and decolonizing anthropology, among others. There are many more Native American scholars entering anthropology and linguistics and they are expanding the disciplines from the inside. Also, there are now several generations of sympathetic anthropologists who

Text continues on page 105

Oregon Native American Language Informants

Name	Language(s) Spoken	Anthropologist/ Linguist	Years Worked with Scholar
Jane & Lizzie Adams	Tillamook	Mandelbaum	1931
John Albert	Alsea	Frachtenburg	1909
Mrs. Emma Bellinger	Yakama	Silverstein	1968
Ida Bensell	Tututni	Pierce	late 1950s/ early 1960s
Laura Bond	Yoncalla	Frachtenburg	1910
Jim Buchanan	Siuslaw	Frachtenburg	1909
Mrs. Ellen Center	Tillamook (Garibaldi-Nehalem dialect)	Boas, Jacobs	1890, 1933
Molale Kate Chantele	Molalla	Jacobs	1920
Amanda Cowan	Klamath	Barker	c. 1960
Charlie Cowen	Klamath	Barrett	1907
Robert David	Klamath	Barker	c. 1960
Ila Dowd	Chinook Jargon	tribal language program	1980s-2002
Frank Drew	Siuslaw	Frachtenburg	1909
Mabie "Neva" Eggsman	Modoc, Klamath	Klamath tribal language program	1980s-2003
Mr. & Mrs. Estabrook	Wasco	Hymes	1971
George Forman	Yakama	Silverstein	1967
Louis Fuller	Tillamook	Jacobs	1920
Alsea George	Alsea	Frachtenburg	1909
Nora Goff	Tillamook	Mandelbaum	1931
William Hartless	Mary's River Kalapuya	Frachtenburg	1910, 1913
Jeff Harney	Siuslaw	Frachtenburg	1909
Molali Henry	Molalla	Frachtenburg	1909
Eustace Howard	Santiam Kalapuya	Frachtenburg	1910
Victoria Howard	Clackamas Chinook	Jacobs	1929, 1930
John (Mose) Hudson Jr.	Santiam Kalapuya, Chinook Jargon	Jacobs	

table continues

Note: Some languages mentioned are not from within Oregon state boundaries but are from closely related languages. The authors want to caution the readers that we make no claims that this list of Oregon Native American language informants is exhaustive. We have tried to be comprehensive, but we acknowledge that the list probably lacks many other people who should be noted. Please contact us so that we may update this list. Please also note that there are multiple spellings for many of these names in both the historical and anthropological literature as well as in archival records.

Name	Language(s) Spoken	Anthropologist/ Linguist	Years Worked with Scholar
Mrs. Susan Jack	Alsea	Frachtenburg	1909
Henry Jackson & his wife	Siuslaw	Frachtenburg	1909
Tom Jackson	Alsea	Frachtenburg	1909
Alex Jefferson	Siuslaw	Frachtenburg	1909
Susie Joe	Umatilla	Rigsby	1960s
Mrs. Alice John	Alsea	Frachtenburg	1909
Doc Johnson	Alsea	Frachtenburg	1909
Martha Johnson	Coos	Ultan	1964
Philip Kahclamat	Wishram	Dyk	1933
James Kashkash	Nez Perce		
L. Kenoyer	Ahantsayuk	Frachtenburg	1910
Louis Kenoy (or Kenuya or Kenoyer)	Yamhill, Twalatin	Jacobs de Angulo & Freeland	1920
Lizzie Kirk	Klamath	Barker	c. 1960
Mary Knighton	Alsea, Kalapuya Molalla	Frachtenburg	1910
Major Lodson	Alsea	Frachtenburg	1909
Mrs. Lodson	Alsea	Frachtenburg	1909
Isaac Martin	Siuslaw	Frachtenburg	1909
Mrs. Isaac Martin	Siuslaw	Frachtenburg	1911
Pete McGuff	Wasco, Wishram	Jacobs	1933
Charlie McKay	Umatilla, Nez Perce	Jacobs	1960s- 1996
Alexander Morrison	Warm Springs	Jacobs	1938
Capt. Numana Gilbert Natchez	N. Paiute	Kroeber	early 1900s
Pansy Ohles	Klamath	Barker	c. 1960
Clara Pearson	Tillamook	Mandelbaum	1931
Annie Miner Peterson	Hanis, Miluk Coos	Jacobs	1933-34
Mr. & Mrs. Grover Pompey	Klamath	Barker	c. 1960
Sargent Sambo	Shasta	Bright	1950
Stevens Savage	Molalla	Frachtenburg	1909, 1910
Mrs. Shontell	Rock Creek Molalla	Frachtenburg	1910
Hoxie Simmons	Tututni	Frachtenburg	1915-16
Louis Simpson	Yakama	Silverstein	1967
Annie Smith	Wasco	Hymes	1971
William Smith	Alsea, Umpqua	Frachtenburg	1909, 1911
Mrs. Mary Stewart	Santiam Kalapuya	Frachtenburg	1910
Jasper Tuftee	Wasco	Hymes	1971
Mrs. Dora Tulee	Yakama	Silverstein	1967

Name	Language(s) Spoken	Anthropologist/ Linguist	Years Worked with Scholar
Mrs. Wallace	Alsea, Kalapuya Molalla	Frachtenburg	1910
Edmond Wheeler	Luckamiut, Yakama	Frachtenburg	1910
Mrs. Grace Wheeler	Kalapuya	Frachtenburg	1910
Jesse Wheeler	Luckamiut	Frachtenburg	1910
Orton Wheeler	Luckamiut	Frachtenburg	1910
Ida White	Yakama	Silverstein	1967
John M. Williams	Molalla	Frachtenburg	1909
Mrs. Kate Williams	Rock Creek Molalla	Frachtenburg	1909, 1910
Elias Williamson	Yoncalla	Frachtenburg	1910
Linton Winishut	Warm Springs	Rigsby	1966
Henry Yelkes	Alsea, Kalapuya Molalla	Frachtenburg	1910

see the benefits of collaborating with Native Americans. In short, the two perspectives are converging.

Issues Regarding Archival Materials

The importance of research collections to Native American language revitalization seems fairly obvious, but there are issues to consider when tribal communities access and use such collections. First, the information that was documented was usually the result of one scientist/linguist working with one Native American informant; thus, the information reflects the bias and interests of the scientist as well as the knowledge of just one person in an entire community. Many social scientists made an effort to talk to the most knowledgeable informants, but the fact remains that any one individual in a community or society will only know a limited amount of information. Thus, only a small fraction of the knowledge available was recorded.

When one takes into consideration the gender of the social scientists and of the informants, it is even more likely that the information recorded is a small percentage of the whole. A male scholar interviewing a male informant may only record words related to a man's activities in that society. Or, if a male interviewed a female, it is unlikely that she would share certain things that should only be told to another female. The backgrounds of both the interviewer and interviewee would also affect what was recorded and why. If the informant was a religious leader, discourse would be weighted towards religious issues; if the interviewer was a missionary, the emphasis may be on language that would help him to convert the Native Americans. Thus, we should not take the information contained in archival collections as the sum total of knowledge that existed at that time, but rather try to understand the possible limitations of the information.

A second limitation of archival materials is related to how the information was recorded. In the archives, we often find that one linguist disagreed with how a previous linguist had transcribed a word, despite the fact that they were both trained to use the International Phonetic alphabet, which aims to negate cross-linguistic orthographic differences. These cross-linguistic differences in orthography are rampant in the work done by non-linguists. A French recorder of Chinook Jargon would use "ou" where an English speaker might use "u" or "oo." Preferred orthographies change over time and often become politically charged.We can see the flexibility in orthography just in the names of Oregon native languages: Molale, Molala, Molalla all represent the same language and no one is left to tell us how the people actually pronounced the name.

In addition, the orthographic system that Native speakers use to record their language is usually the orthography of the Euro-American languages through which they learned literacy skills. However, Native American languages contain several sounds that do not exist in European languages, so the fit is not good. Eventually, as speakers of the Native language became dominant in English, they begin to pronounce Native sounds more like the English sounds represented by a particular letter. For example, the Inupiaq phoneme /p/ is a sound that is actually a cross between the English /b/ and /p/, but because English is the first language spoken today by many Inupiaq peoples and the letter "p" is used in Inupiaq orthography, the Inupiaq /p/ is beginning to be pronounced like the English /p/. Other times the Native transcriber may get confused using English letters. While working with a 1981 place-name list from her own community (the King Island Inupiaq Eskimo), Kingston learned that the person who had recorded the names, a King Island elder trained to write the Inupiaq language, often transposed the letters "k" and "q," which represent the same sound in English. However, in Inupiaq, the two letters represent two different phonemes, a sound like the English "k" and a glottal sound produced farther back in the throat. Kingston was lucky because the linguist who had worked on the list (Lawrence D. Kaplan) knew that the elder often transposed these letters. In many cases, no one living would know either the social scientist or the informant, so idiosyncrasies in spelling may never come to light.

Another issue to consider is that all languages change through time. Sometimes the changes are internal to the language and can't be explained through contact with other languages. Languages also borrow from each other. So, for instance, if a tribe has archival materials on their language from fifty years ago, seventy-five years ago, and one hundred years ago, can any one be considered the "pristine" or "correct" version? Should the one recorded by some white social scientist one hundred years ago be considered "more correct" than the one that elders now speak? The variety spoken today likely shows the results of language contact and change over the generations, but language is a living instrument.

Another problem with how language was recorded has to do with changing technologies. Many Native American languages in Oregon were recorded on reel-to-reel tapes and some even exist on old wax cylinders. Playback machines for these technologies are no longer made and, even if they do exist, the fragile nature of the recordings themselves often dictates whether or not the recordings can be used or accessed. Specialty laboratories that can make audiotape or digital tape duplicates of these recordings exist, but are often prohibitively expensive. Another consideration in making duplicates is using technology that promises to be used into the future. CD-ROM format is currently the best archival solution, but one hundred years ago, the standard was wax cylinder, then vinyl records, then reel-to-reel tape, and then cassette tapes.

Another struggle for tribal archivists lies in creating and managing an archive that is accessible to community members. Issues include finding and gathering the materials, funding the archives, organizing the materials, making decisions on the restrictions that should be placed on archival materials, and deciding where to house materials in order to make them both safe and accessible to interested parties. Just finding the materials pertinent to a community can be difficult and involves a large investment of time and money over a period of years. Much of the material Kingston has found on King Island has been by pure accident, like going to the New Bedford Whaling Museum in Massachusetts and seeing King Island masks hanging on display. After the Associated Press ran a story about her King Island research in early 2004, people who lived or worked in Nome in the mid-twentieth century called and wrote to her and offered copies of photographs of King Islanders. As much as a tribe might wish to be systematic in their research, they must also be open to getting copies of materials through pure accident. Even creating an interest in these materials in tribal communities can be a significant obstacle, because of the history behind their creation as well as the time that must be invested in learning how to use them.

Funding for tribal language programs and tribal archives is often quite scarce, as tribes often have more pressing needs, such as health care, unemployment, and housing. If a tribe seeks federal funding for their archive, that archive then must comply with the Freedom of Information Act (FOI), which dictates that anything that is federally funded must be made accessible to any U.S. citizen, whether tribal or not. If a tribe wants to assert their sovereignty and only allow archival access to their own tribal members, it will violate FOI and become ineligible for potential federal monies.

Another issue is how the materials should be organized. Should the tribe use the organizational scheme and categories used by non-Indian archivists? This often emphasizes a strict chronology or categories that make sense to the scholar, but usually do not reflect how Native Americans might organize or categorize these materials. Or, should tribes use an organizational scheme that reflects Indian culture more closely? Myra Johnson of the Confederated Tribes of Warm Springs suggested that organizing materials according to season might be more culturally appropriate and useful to tribal members.

Other questions arise. What kind of restrictions should the tribe place on archival materials that contain sensitive information or on materials that have deteriorated? How does a tribe make these materials accessible to interested tribal members without offending others? Where should materials be housed? How should a tribe get the funds to build and maintain archival-quality facilities for their materials? Should the tribe pay for a full-time archivist? How does one get other tribal people interested in looking through these materials? Why should tribes be interested in these materials? How can these materials be used for language instruction? These are all questions to consider when creating and maintaining an archive for tribal community uses.

Existing Native American Tribal Archives in Oregon

As stated above, many tribal authorities often state that their elders are their language archives. For some Native American languages, those with many speakers, this is indeed the truth. But for most of Oregon's Native American languages, the truth is that there are no living speakers, or very few, and that the languages have no chance of being revived without the data in archives.

Linguistic collections in Oregon exist mainly in tribal cultural and educational institutions. This is because members of Oregon's Native American tribes have worked very hard to repatriate these materials to Oregon in the past twenty years. A few, namely the Coquille Indian Tribe and the Confederated Tribes of Umatilla, have created publicly accessible libraries for research. The Coquille Indian Tribal Library is located in the tribe's administrative office in North Bend and contains information on a number of tribes in southwest Oregon. It is part of the Coos County library system. The Confederated Tribes of Umatilla have housed their collections, including archival and photographic materials, as well as artifacts, in their cultural center, the Tamastslikt Cultural Institute in Pendleton.

Most other tribes have not yet created a public access feature to their collections, although some, such as the Confederated Tribes of Warm Springs, have started the process of developing a public access policy. The Museum at Warm Springs does have a permanent collection of artifacts, historic photographs, murals, graphics, and rare documents. The Warm Springs' Culture and Heritage Department also has photographs, audio and video recordings, and maps. The Confederated Tribes of Grand Ronde; the Confederated Tribes of Siletz; the Klamath Tribes; the Burns Paiute; Confederated Tribes of Coos, Lower Umpqua, and Siuslaw; and the Cow Creek Indian Tribe are all actively engaged in acquiring archival documents, but these collections are generally not accessible to the general public. Most tribes do have some of the collections accessible to their tribal members or the tribal public.

The Southwest Oregon Research Project and Collection
In 1995, the Coquille Indian Tribe initiated the Southwest Oregon Research Project (SWORP) that serves to enhance the archival language collections of all tribes in Oregon and offers a public access component as well. The SWORP model works through collaborations with the University of Oregon and the Smithsonian Institution, where more than 110,000 pages of archival materials have been found and returned to Oregon. These are a mixture of ethnographic materials, government data and correspondence, and Native American languages. In fact, the greatest proportion of ethnographic materials is related to Oregon Native American languages.

Many tribes have used similar records in support of sovereignty. This is clearly the case for all of the tribes that applied or are applying for federal restoration or recognition as it is necessary to assemble a paper record of continuous cultural practices for the federal application. This characteristic of the SWORP collection is emphasized by both George Wasson and Jason Younker when they write about the "paper proof" of the SWORP materials. The SWORP collection is an assemblage of the documents that document the existence of Oregon tribes and prove the rights of Oregon tribes to be federally recognized.

George Wasson (Coquille/University of Oregon) initiated the first SWORP field research project in Washington, D.C., in the summer of 1995. Wasson had been working with the Smithsonian Institution for many years and developed the idea of bringing the documents back to Oregon. Researchers from the University of Oregon's Department of Anthropology and from the Coquille Indian Tribe went to the Smithsonian Institution, skimmed through the manuscripts in the National Anthropological Archives and marked those to be copied and returned to Oregon. The SWORP team defined their project boundary as southwestern Oregon, centered on the Coquille Tribe, and copied documents directly related to that region. The researchers brought back approximately sixty thousand pages of information in the form of paper copies, microfilm, and maps from the National Anthropological Archives and National Archives. Photographic and audiotape collections were later added to the collection.

As a result of the successful project, the Coquille Tribe and the University of Oregon had a potlatch giveaway in May 1997 where five western Oregon Tribes (Siletz, Grand Ronde, Cow Creek, Coos Lower Umpqua Siuslaw, and Coquille) and two northern California tribes (Smith River Rancheria and Elk Valley Rancheria) received copies of the SWORP collection.

The SWORP effort proved so successful that in 1998 Mark Tveskov (University of Oregon) and Jason Younker (Coquille/University of Oregon) coordinated SWORP II field research in Washington, D.C. The research team during SWORP II was made up of individuals from four Oregon tribes: Deni Hockema and Amanda Mitchell from the Coquille Tribe, Patty Whereat (Director of Cultural Resources of the Coos Tribe), Robert Kentta (Director of Cultural Resources of Siletz), and David Lewis from Grand Ronde. Hockema and Lewis were then graduate students at the University of Oregon. Tveskov coordinated the team in Washington, D.C., where they spent six weeks at the National Anthropological Archives and the National Archives, College Park, Maryland. SWORP II had an expanded project region that included northern California and southwestern Washington and this yielded approximately fifty thousand pages of paper copies from the three repositories.

The Inventory to the SWORP Collection was published by the University of Oregon Knight Library in June 2001. On June 9th, 2001, the Coquille Indian Tribe and University of Oregon initiated the second potlatch, where seventeen tribes from greater Oregon were given copies of relevant manuscripts from SWORP and forty-four tribes were given copies of the published inventory to the collection. The seventeen unique copies of the collection were finished in May 2002 and delivered to the tribes.

The SWORP collection is stored in fifty acid-free archival boxes at the University of Oregon, which makes these records readily accessible to Native American people and to scholars of Oregon Native American ethnohistory. There are approximately 110,000 pages (accumulating from SWORP I and SWORP II) in the collection and the records date from the 1850s to the 1950s. The collection covers a region encompassing southwestern Washington, western Oregon, and northern California that is the traditional homeland for about forty-four federally recognized tribes. Linguistic manuscripts alone contain information from more than eighty Native American languages throughout the Americas, many of which are extinct or severely endangered. The scope of the language manuscripts in SWORP, which include linguistic discussions, vocabulary lists, vocabulary comparisons, theory discussions, and publication manuscripts, may hold relevance to every tribe in North America. The diversity of languages represented in the collection is the result of the early efforts of scholars to compare native languages from many different regions attempting to find similarities between them, to find families of languages, and to eventually track the historic expansion of people across the continents (North and South America).

The SWORP collection is unique because it was created by Native American people, effectively reversing the colonization process by returning or "repatriating" indigenous intellectual knowledge to the descendants of the original culture and heritage bearers.

Major ethnographers and their areas of study in the SWORP Collection:

Alexander Anderson	Crescent City, Tolowa
Franz Boas	Chinook
Jeremiah Curtin	Klamath River, CA
James Dorsey	Siletz
Philip Drucker	Tolowa, Oregon Coast
Leo Frachtenberg	Siletz, Grand Ronde
Albert Gatschet	Grand Ronde, Klamath
George Gibbs	Grand Ronde, Chinook J.
Harry St. Clair	Siletz
Thomas T. Waterman	S.W. Oregon, N. California
James Wickersham	Chinook

A personal story (David Lewis)

In the summer of 1998, I was fortunate to join the SWORP II team of researchers that went to Washington, D.C., for six weeks sifting through archives to find records related to western Oregon tribes. This research may be the single most important experience of my years as a student. I did not know what to expect, if I would like the work, or whether we would find anything significant. I found that my personal interests resonated well with archival research. I was able to find records that few people had looked at for over one hundred years—records, letters, and photographs that were written about and by people directly in my bloodlines.

I began to realize that government records, for Native American people, are actually a part of our genealogical records. Since then, I have found this true for many published government documents. For instance, the Congressional Serial Set contains annual reports of my tribe and reservation, reports, censuses, and details about our people, reports not produced in the same detail or quantity about any other ethnic group in the United States. One of the most amazing "finds" I came across in the National Archives in downtown Washington, D.C., was a letter from the Siletz Reservation that contained a packet of flour within it. This letter had never been opened by the Commissioner of Indian Affairs, and I had it opened at the research desk in the National Archives. The complete package had a letter, a separate packet of flour, untouched, inside. When we viewed the letter and packet, some of the one-hundred-year-old flour leaked out on the desk. The letter articulated that the Siletz Indians had sent this flour to the commissioner to prove the high quality of the flour being produced on the reservation. Since the letter had not been opened, this message was not heard by the commissioner. Maybe someday, someone will repatriate the flour.

Archival research is an amazing process of discovery and rediscovery. We had read about how Indian people were put in boarding schools, but to read letters by our family about how their children were kidnapped and kept at the schools and not allowed to return home creates another level of interaction with this history. And the fact that these letters were written by Native American people adds another level of understanding. Within one generation of being moved to the reservation, my ancestors could read and write in English. And they were incredibly brave to speak out against the policies of the Indian Agents on the reservation, even though most of their food and resources came through the agent.

Finally, to be able to work with so many other great Native American researchers, people who were already working on cultural issues that I was just learning about, was enlightening. I believe we all came away from that summer with some great experiences, and we certainly created a collection of documents that maybe someday will help to correct histories written about our peoples and help restore cultural ways long out of practice.

Archives in the State

The availability of Oregon Native American language resources usually depends on whether there was a linguist or anthropologist who worked on such subjects. Joe E. Pierce was an anthropologist at Portland State University through the mid-twentieth century. Pierce worked on the Siletz Reservation and created reel-to-reel recordings of Tolowa and Tututni languages spoken there. At one point, these recordings were transferred to cassette tapes, copies of which are now held at the Oregon State University (OSU) archives. OSU Archives now has an Internet-searchable database called "The Oregon Multicultural Archives" (http://osulibrary.oregonstate.edu/archives/oma/), including materials on Native Americans. OSU Archives was also one of the lead institutions in the creation of the Northwest Digital Archives project, another Internet-searchable database of the holdings of various archival institutions in the Pacific Northwest (http://nwda.wsulibs.wsu.edu/). The final archive of importance in Oregon is the Oregon Historical Society, which possesses some resources, mainly published documentation, but its focus is on history and not necessarily language. Their unique language materials are primarily related to out-of-state languages. Other scholars have worked on Oregon Native American languages at various Oregon institutions, which may hold their papers or original sound recordings in their archives or libraries.

Some government records for the Indian reservations (Grand Ronde and Siletz) are located in Oregon, in the SWORP collection (http://gladstone.uoregon.edu/~coyotez/), which includes the Congressional Serial Set (limited to reports to Congress and House), as well as in Oregon Territorial records in microfilm archives at the major Oregon research libraries. There are some Oregon Indian records in the Oregon State Archives (http://www.sos.state.or.us/), but these resources are limited as Indian Affairs was a federal responsibility. In the past decade, there has been a growing government-to-government relationship between the Oregon Native American tribes and the state of Oregon. This relationship may produce some agreements about

Oregon Native American languages. State records are mainly in the Oregon State Archives, the Oregon State Library (http://oregon.gov/ OSL/), and at the major universities.

Out-of-State Archives

As listed in Appendix One, many archival repositories outside of Oregon maintain large Oregon language collections. In addition, the primary repositories for government collections are the National Archives and Records Administration in Washington, D.C., and College Park, Maryland, as well as the regional archives in San Bruno, California, and Sand Point, Washington. For ethnohistoric records, the list is much longer, with the National Anthropological Archives in Maryland the most prominent.

Government records can help to establish the context for the reservations for each year that records were produced, especially in the early years of the reservation. Tribes were under intense stresses to stop practicing their culture and speaking their languages and the government programs were the primary stressors. Boarding and day schools were under the control of the government and there are annual records of the students showing their progress towards "civilization." In addition, there is extensive correspondence from Indian agents, employees of the reservations, and Native Americans, discussing many of the problems at the reservation.

The stresses placed on Native Americans at the reservation were magnified by the racism projected on Indians by the surrounding American society. For example, Indians were paid one half the salaries of white men or women for the same job. This situation is documented in the annual reservation accounting reports that clearly show the salary and ethnicity of each employee at the reservation. The stresses of simply being an Indian caused many Native Americans to find ways to stop living like an Indian: by moving to the cities, by dressing as whites, and by ceasing to speak their languages. This is documented in the archival materials held by these institutions.

Internet Resources

In the past fifteen years there has been significant growth in Internet resources for language researchers. There are listserves, papers, essays, theses, blogs, and whole manuscripts available in various formats on the Internet. One of the most extensive of these resources is the LinguistList listserve (http://linguistlist.org/) that includes individual listserves on most major indigenous languages. All of the messages are archived on the site in a fully searchable format. The

Summer Institute of Linguistics (http://www.ethnologue.com/web. asp) also has extensive resources available to language researchers. At the University of Oregon, the Yamada Language Center (http:// babel.uoregon.edu/yamada/fonts.html) houses the most extensive downloadable indigenous fonts inventory on the Internet. Also at the University of Oregon, Professor Scott Delancey's language Web pages are a very good survey of Native American languages in Oregon (http://www.uoregon.edu/~delancey/links/linglinks.html). Don Macnaughtan at Lane Community College has established an extensive bibliographic Web page of Oregon language resources and their archival locations (http://www.lanecc.edu/library/don/index. htm). In 2006 the SWORP inventory was added to the Northwest Digital Archives database (http://nwda.wsulibs.wsu.edu/).

The repositories that have the primary collections are now establishing online profiles for accessing those collections. One good example is the University of Washington, where Kalapuya Texts is now publicly accessible (http://www.lib.washington.edu/types/texts/ K.html). The best overall place to search for such resources is the Library of Congress digital collections Web site (http://international. loc.gov/intldl/find/digital_collections.html), which links to many other sites.

Perhaps the most extensive Internet representation of any one Oregon Native American language is Chinook Jargon. Primarily operating through the Chinook-L listserve on LinguistList, Chinook Jargon has developed international scholar groups with members in Canada, Germany, Spain, and various states within the United States. There are several Web pages containing links to full Chinook Jargon dictionaries and other educational and organizational resources.

The next well-developed language resource is Phil Cash Cash's Indigenous Language and Technology (ILAT) listserve operating out of the University of Arizona (http://www.u.arizona.edu/~cashcash/). The ILAT listserve features daily indigenous-language development and education news as well as discussion among some of the most prominent Native American language scholars from throughout the world. It specializes in news and information on new technological developments to aid tribal language workers and scholars. Along with this is Cash Cash's personal Web site containing extensive information and links related to his research on Eastern Oregon languages, in particular Nez Perce.[17]

New sites highlighting Native languages come online occasionally, such as the impressive work of Philip Spaelti. Spaelti, who teaches in Kobe, Japan, has created an electronically searchable version of Barker's Klamath dictionary that is much easier to use.

Conclusion

There is a wealth of information on Oregon Native American languages held in archives across the state of Oregon and across the nation. This valuable information, often recorded by ethnographers and linguists in the past under difficult circumstances from Native American peoples, is gradually becoming more and more accessible to Native American tribes and peoples interested in revitalizing their languages. This is due primarily to the efforts of the Native American tribal peoples themselves who are repatriating these records to their own libraries and archives. Their efforts are helped by those non-Native scholars who recognize that this information represents the intellectual property of Native American peoples and are working to make this information more accessible to them. It is a difficult road, though. In order to access and use these collections, Native Americans must first find the records, obtain proper rights to use the information, understand the historical context under which the material was recorded (which includes knowing the different orthographies used for each language and how and in what ways the knowledge might be limited), have the appropriate equipment to play any audio recordings of their languages (including wax cylinders, reel-to-reel tapes, records, tape cassettes, etc.), and make hard decisions about which materials to use in the classroom and how those materials should be presented. It will take patience, persistence, and dedication to find and use this information, but doing so recognizes the sacrifices of those have gone before.

There is certainly movement toward the positive in Oregon, as in the past few years laws have been passed that favor Oregon Native American languages and archives. Oregon State House Bill 2674 was signed by the governor on May 25th, 2005.[18] This was the result of the Oregon Collaborative Project, which was organized by the Oregon State Libraries Association and the Confederated Tribes of the Umatilla, Tamastslikt Cultural Center, through the efforts of Malissa Minthorn. This house bill essentially categorizes tribal libraries as public libraries and allows them to apply for public library grants and to gain services through the Oregon State Library system. This improves the access to the documented research that has been done on Oregon Native languages. Both teachers and learners stand to benefit from easier access to the words of their ancestors.

Chapter Five

Best Practices in Language Teaching

Juan Antonio Trujillo

Introduction

This chapter approaches language-revitalization efforts from an applied-linguistics perspective. Applied linguistics is an academic field of study in which researchers explore ways that linguistic theory can help address real-world concerns. Among the issues addressed by applied linguists are second language acquisition and the preservation of ancestral languages. It is an interdisciplinary field that incorporates resources from other areas as needed, drawing frequently on educational theory and technology.

There has often been a reluctance on the part of tribal language and culture program directors to spend time reading the research published by applied linguists in journals and books. It is true that much of the work done by linguists is presented in a technical format that seems very detached and mechanical to people who experience language loss on a more visceral, emotional level. Unfortunately, language loss is not a limited phenomenon. James Crawford, executive director of the National Association for Bilingual Education, speaks of a "worldwide crisis," and cites figures indicating that as many as half of the world's six thousand languages are at serious risk.[1] The body of knowledge that has been developed over the years by applied linguists includes the experiences of colonized people all over the world who are going through the same struggles as the tribes in Oregon.

We will begin with an overview of developments in the recent history of language education, some thoughts about current educational philosophy, and a discussion of the potential role of national proficiency-oriented content standards in programs designed for learners of indigenous languages. Finally, we will move beyond the strictly educational aspects of applied linguistics in order to examine some additional insights that language theory can offer to individual learners, language instructors, and program planners.

The Changing Scope of Language Teaching

For many years, language programs in schools and universities focused on teaching vocabulary lists and explaining grammar structures. Teachers expected students to be able to translate classical literary texts, analyze sentences, and reproduce vocabulary lists. Very little emphasis was placed on being able to create original sentences or engage in real communication with native speakers of the language being learned. In fact, before the twentieth century, schools seldom had instruction in modern languages available at all, preferring classical Latin and Greek.

It was not until the end of World War II and the onset of the Cold War that U.S. government agencies fully recognized the advantages that could be gained by having large numbers of people in diplomatic and military service who were capable of engaging in fluent interaction with people anywhere there was a perceived strategic interest. This shift in priorities, together with advances in the field of educational psychology, led to many more languages being offered for study and to the development of language-teaching approaches centered on communicative proficiency rather than grammar and translation. Although some rather repetitive activities remained popular (pattern drills, memorization of dialogues, etc.), class time was much more clearly devoted to activities that experts of one persuasion or another believed would lead to an ability to understand and create authentic language.

By the late 1950s and early 1960s, linguistics was emerging as an important academic discipline in American universities. Perhaps most prominent among the linguists of that period was Noam Chomsky,[2] whose transformational model shifted the attention of American linguists away from historical studies and toward research into how language itself functions at a single moment in time. However, Chomsky's work continued to focus on grammar. Among the first scholars to reject the narrow, grammar-centric approach to language study was Dell Hymes, a linguistic anthropologist who spent many years working with Oregon's indigenous-language communities. Recognizing that knowing when to say something is just as important as knowing how to say it, Hymes proposed a view of language that takes into account a number of social or cultural variables. Hymes referred to the combination of grammatical knowledge and cultural understanding needed to communicate effectively as *communicative competence*.[3]

Michael Canale and Merrill Swain later described how the notion of communicative competence works in the second-language classroom.[4] They identified four main components: 1) *grammatical competence*, or command of the rules of language; 2) *sociolinguistic competence*, or understanding of the social dimensions of communication; 3) *discourse competence*, or the ability to put ideas into a cohesive form; and 4) *strategic competence*, or proficiency with verbal and nonverbal tools that increase the speaker's ability to achieve whatever end goal was intended. More simply stated, it doesn't matter that a student knows how to say grammatically something if he or she doesn't know when to say it, why to say it, or to whom it should be said. This type of knowledge comes only from an intimate understanding of the cultural context in which the language is normally used.

As a result of this expanded understanding of what effective communication entails, cultural information, role playing, and later authentic problem solving began to play an increasingly prominent role in textbooks and other teaching materials. This period of research also marked the beginning of another critical expansion of the boundaries of the language-learning profession, one that eventually led to the 1996 publication of *Standards for Foreign Language Learning,* which will be addressed in some detail later.

Despite the changes brought about during the postwar period, language instruction in the United States is still primarily thought of as a way for native English speakers to interact with foreigners while living, working, or traveling outside the country. What learners need to know under these circumstances is somewhat predictable—it starts with basic survival skills involving food, shelter, and transportation, then gradually turns to tasks and vocabulary related to specific recreational or vocational pursuits. Nearly all current beginning textbooks, regardless of the language being taught, still dedicate a considerable number of pages to travel and recreation-related tasks while simultaneously highlighting, and even exaggerating, stark contrasts between the culture of the learner—presumed to be fundamentally Euro-American—and the traditional beliefs and practices of people living overseas.

The true relationship between language learners and the language being learned is far more complex, particularly when indigenous languages are involved. Although it is true that global transportation systems now make international travel accessible to more than just the most economically privileged, the contact language learners in Oregon schools are most likely to have with other languages will increasingly be in their home towns. Furthermore, as the population continues to diversify, increasingly more students will belong to ethnic or cultural groups that claim something other than English as a traditional or heritage language.

The increase in population diversity is still only part of the reason that the traditional second-language curriculum may fail to meet the needs of today's language students. In failing to recognize that second languages are more likely to be encountered in a domestic setting than in an international one, current language-teaching strategies also fail to take into account the tremendous pressure that heritage-language students feel to prefer English. Even in the Spanish-speaking population, which continues to be fed at a rapid pace by fresh monolingual non-English-speaking immigrants, research shows a rapid shift to English that begins immediately upon arrival and is essentially complete by the second or third generation.[5] If current trends in language preference continue, most heritage language learners, like Native American students today, will be fluent speakers of English who hear their traditional language in an increasingly limited number of public spaces.

The implications of these observations are clear. Second-language learners are increasingly joined in the classroom by native speakers of languages other than English, as well as by heritage learners who are not fluent, but who have a historical and psychological connection to the language being studied. As a result, language learners in the twenty-first century will have need of linguistic skills related to home and community more than they will require assistance learning to travel abroad. They will need strategies to help them maintain a sense of identity as they learn to navigate through a complex, multicultural environment more than lessons on how to get by while spending time as guests in another country. Especially in the case of groups that have historically been targets of discrimination, they will also require tools to help them lead their communities toward greater social and economic empowerment in the face of strong pressure to assimilate. A curriculum that does not meet these needs will not lead to successful language revitalization. Fortunately, the language-teaching profession seems to be moving in a positive direction.

New Directions: The National Standards Project

Following the publication of the landmark 1983 report by the National Commission on Excellence in Education, *A Nation at Risk*, educational planning took center stage in a number of professional organizations. Among the groups that initiated work on a complete revision of the country's educational agenda was the American Council on the Teaching of Foreign Languages (ACTFL). Working in collaboration with the nation's largest professional societies for language teachers, ACTFL published a set of learning standards in 1996 that redefined the content of the foreign-language curriculum. The new standards, commonly referred to as the "Five Cs," stake out the broadest view yet of what it means to study language (see figure 5.1). Although the standards, for the sake of tradition, regrettably maintain the use of the term "foreign" to refer to languages other than English, careful reading of the standards shows that its authors do indeed recognize the multilingual, multicultural nature of the environment in which our learners operate. The standards address a nation of learners who are expected to have local access to people whose language and culture differ from their own. This is certainly a step in the right direction.

As the standards work their way into official educational policy at the national level, a more nuanced depiction of the relationship between different curricular elements is emerging. Although second

Figure 5.1 Standards for Foreign Language Learning

1. Communication: Communicate in Languages Other Than English

1.1 Students engage in conversations, provide and obtain information, express feelings and emotions, and exchange opinions.
1.2 Students understand and interpret written and spoken language on a variety of topics.
1.3 Students present information, concepts, and ideas to an audience of listeners or readers on a variety of topics.

2. Cultures: Gain Knowledge and Understanding of Other Cultures

2.1 Students demonstrate an understanding of the relationship between the practices and perspectives of the culture studied.
2.2 Students demonstrate an understanding of the relationship between the products and perspectives of the cultures studied.

3. Connections: Connect with Other Disciplines and Acquire Information

3.1 Students reinforce and further their knowledge of other disciplines through the foreign language.
3.2 Students acquire information and recognize the distinctive viewpoints that are only available through the foreign language and its cultures.

4. Comparisons: Developing Insight into the Nature of Language and Culture

4.1 Students demonstrate understanding of the nature of language through comparisons of the language studied and their own.
4.2 Students demonstrate understanding of the concept of culture through comparisons of the cultures studied and their own.

5. Communities: Participate in Multilingual Communities at Home and Around the World

5.1 Students use the language both within and beyond the school setting.
5.2 Students show evidence of becoming life-long learners by using the language for personal enjoyment and enrichment.

Source: National Standards in Foreign Language Education Project (1996). *Standards for Foreign Language Learning*, p. 9.

language programs have yet to become a formal part of the National Assessment of Educational Progress (NAEP), a testing framework has been developed that firmly places interpersonal, interpretive, and presentational communication at the center of the curriculum. As seen in figure 5.2, the remaining four Cs (Cultures, Comparisons, Connection, and Communities) are envisioned as secondary elements that form the context in which communication takes place.

The standards are useful because they promote a common vision for the language-teaching profession and introduce a common vocabulary for talking about what language teaching entails. However, they were never intended to be used on the local level as a finished product. It is still up to individual policy-making bodies like local school districts to flesh out just how the broad vision of the standards should look for them. Ideally, each language program should be able to translate the broad standards into very specific, measurable goals. For example, when the standards include "Students understand and interpret written and spoken language on a variety of topics," tribal language program leadership would want to decide what topics each course in the program should cover, what kinds of written or spoken language are most important at each level, and how instructors will measure whether each student's level of understanding is enough to move on. From community to community, the answers may be very different. In cases like the reservation setting, where the curricular goals may be more about cultural and linguistic revitalization than about the linguistic achievements of individual students, the NAEP model that strongly emphasizes communication over the remaining Cs may require some re-evaluation.

Figure 5.2. Source: National Assessment Governing Board (2000). *Framework for the 2004 foreign language National Assessment of Educational Progress.* Available online: http://www.nagb.org/pubs/FinalFrameworkPrePubEdition1.pdf

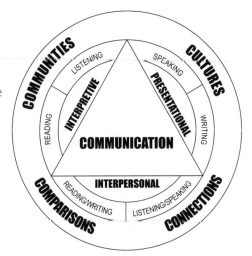

For Native American learners of traditional languages, and indeed for the increasingly large number of heritage-language learners who hail from other communities with a non-Anglophone history, even broader modifications to the content defined in the National Standards may be in order. One idea that illustrates how this might work is a sixth content standard that has been implemented recently in Spanish courses at Oregon State University in order to address the issue of cultural empowerment for language communities that have been subjected to discriminatory treatment by English-centered power structures. The wording goes something like this—see Figure 5.3.

Figure 5.3

6. Consciousness: Recognize Your Role in Systems of Privilege and Promote Equity

6.1 Students recognize the role of language and culture in systems of privilege and oppression.
6.2 Students use language and culture to promote equity and social justice.

Readers familiar with the field of educational theory will recognize in these statements the influence of Paolo Freire, a Brazilian educational theorist who was well acquainted with the effects of institutional racism and economic disparity in public education. Freire's seminal *Pedagogy of the Oppressed* explains that a primary task of public education should be what he terms *conscientização*, or assisting learners to arrive at an awareness of their role in systems of social and economic oppression. This consciousness raising then sets the stage for personal liberation and a dedication to bringing about a just and equitable society for all.

The framers of the National Standards might question the addition of another content area at the national level, particularly one that appears so politically charged. However, taking into account the new multicultural and multilingual face of the twenty-first-century learner whose needs have been marginalized by the educational establishment for so long, this is at the very least a discussion that ought not be neglected by language professionals. As Richard Shaull states in his foreword to *Pedagogy of the Oppressed*:

> There is no such thing as a neutral educational process.
> Education either functions as an instrument that is used to
> facilitate the integration of the younger generation into the
> logic of the present system and bring about conformity to
> it, or it becomes the "practice of freedom," the means by
> which men and women ... discover how to participate in the
> transformation of their world.[6]

If it is true, as the NAEP authors suggest, that cultures, comparisons, connections, and communities provide the context in which communication happens, it is equally evident to the politically conscious educator that all of those activities in turn take place within an even broader context that is defined by political and economic power structures. The Consciousness goal could then be represented on the NAEP framework as shown in figure 5.4.

Civic engagement is not typically addressed in language-learning publications despite its increasing relevance to the language learner, but a review of resources available outside the language profession suggest that the language-learning environment is highly compatible with the conditions needed to create socially engaged learners. Public policy expert Mary Kirlin identifies four primary skills needed for effective civic engagement: collective decision making; communication; critical thinking; and organization.[7] Communication and critical thinking are certainly covered in the national language curriculum, and a well-run language program will provide ample opportunity for students to learn to work in teams, organize daily activities, and participate in special events for school or community groups. The language program can indeed be one of the most empowering spaces at a school or community center.

Language-Teaching Methods

The National Standards define, in broad terms, what language professionals believe the content of a good language program should include. They do not, however, dictate what method should be used to help learners meet those broad content objectives, nor do

Figure 5.4

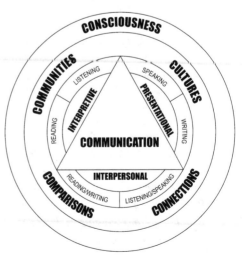

they define steps along the path to proficiency. An examination of language-teaching approaches shows that recent methods involving contextualized, task-based activities and integrated, authentic assessment come much closer to providing what the heritage learner needs than the rigid, memorization-intensive activities of previous decades.

Most students in tribal language programs have already learned a first language—usually English. We will address the differences between first- and second-language learning a bit further on. For now, let us stipulate that a child's first language is generally learned without the need of formal instruction or classes of any kind, and second-language learning typically involves a more hands-on approach. Schools and universities have tried an astounding array of techniques to teach language. Grammar-translation, discussed at the beginning of this chapter, relies heavily on explanations of grammar and memorization of vocabulary and has been used for centuries. More recent approaches attempt to simulate the learning process of children and avoid grammar explanations entirely (Direct Method), and others treat language as a set of habits or responses that can be made automatic through repetition (Audiolingual Method). Still others attempt to involve the subconscious mind (Suggestopedia), stimulate the entire body (Total Physical Response), or emulate the recovery process used in group therapy (Community Language Learning).[8] With such a broad array of methods at our disposal and taking into account the near-religious fervor with which some instructors adhere to one approach or another, it is no wonder that defining a curriculum at the school district or tribal level can be a serious institutional challenge.

On the one hand, it is useful for teachers to have some knowledge of the full range of language-teaching strategies that have been used over the centuries. It allows them to pick and choose activities to meet the different needs that may arise with particular groups of learners. On the other hand, each of the methods and approaches listed above is tied to a specific educational philosophy, and those philosophies are sometimes mutually exclusive. Methods that rely heavily on repetition come from the belief that language learning is essentially a more sophisticated version of the famous experiment with Pavlov's dog—a conditioned response to external stimuli. Methods that shun grammar explanations in favor of controlled practice of increasingly complex structures are based on the belief that languages are based on principles and rules that learners discover on their own as they process information internally. It's not likely that either philosophy correctly and completely describes how we learn language, and it may be some time before science can provide an answer.

One of the more popular approaches to educational philosophy in Oregon in recent years is the model known as constructivism. Jerome S. Bruner, the American psychologist credited with developing constructivist theory in the twentieth century, was also an authority on the acquisition of language.[9] The basic premise of constructivism is that learners come to the classroom with a mental framework that explains the world as they have experienced it. As they are exposed to new information and experiences, they re-evaluate and repeatedly reconstruct that mental framework. In a constructivist classroom, the role of the teacher is not to feed facts to the learners for them to regurgitate later, but rather to set up situations in which students can encounter new ideas and work together to figure out how they fit in with their previous knowledge. This is, of course, one of many competing educational models, but one that seems particularly compatible with the growing evidence that teaching language within a natural context leads to greater success in creating real speakers.

The proficiency-oriented, constructivist learning environment also helps teachers meet the needs of more students. Activities based on rote learning and translation favor students who think and learn in a highly formalized way that has long been valued by Western cultures. However, educators are finally coming to the realization that there are many types of knowledge, and that good teaching will provide students opportunities to succeed in their personal areas of intellectual strength. Howard Gardner proposed an initial listing of several different "intelligences" in 1983. They include linguistic, logical-mathematical, musical, bodily-kinesthetic, spatial, interpersonal, and intrapersonal.[10] These dimensions of knowledge, as well as others that have been proposed since the publication of Gardner's original work, are often valued differently by people from diverse cultural backgrounds. A program that is built around solid constructivist principles will respond far better to individual and community needs than a program that follows the authoritarian academic model most of us were exposed to as children.

Re-orienting the Curriculum toward Proficiency

One thing that most language educators and educational administrators can now agree on is that we want the students to leave language programs with an ability to communicate. Once there is agreement that communicative proficiency is the goal of the language program, the selection of a method or set of methods becomes easier. Alice

Omaggio Hadley, a proponent of proficiency-centered language instruction, formulated a set of guidelines—she refers to them as "hypotheses"—that provide an excellent yardstick for deciding whether any given method or type of classroom activity is likely to lead to proficiency. See Figure 5.5 below.

Let's take a typical exercise used in a traditional elementary-school language class and show how it could be modified to better address the goals listed in figure 5.5. For this activity, assume that the instructor has prepared a set of related vocabulary items—forest animals, let's say—on a set of large flashcards. The front of each card shows a picture of the animal, and the back of the card has the name of the animal printed in the target language. For a ten-minute period, the instructor shows pictures, waits for the class to respond, then shows the back of the card with the printed name of the animal while modeling the correct pronunciation.

Figure 5.5

Hypothesis 1. Opportunities must be provided for students to practice using language in a range of contexts likely to be encountered in the target culture.

Corollary 1. Students should be encouraged to express their own meaning as early as possible after productive skills have been introduced in the course of instruction.
Corollary 2. Opportunities must be provided for active communicative interaction among students.
Corollary 3. Creative language practice (as opposed to exclusively manipulative or convergent practice) must be encouraged in the proficiency-oriented classroom.
Corollary 4. Authentic language should be used in instruction wherever possible.

Hypothesis 2. Opportunities should be provided for students to practice carrying out a range of function (tasks) likely to be necessary in dealing with others in the target culture.

Hypothesis 3. The development of accuracy should be encouraged in proficiency-oriented instruction. As learners produce language, various forms of instruction and evaluative feedback can be useful in facilitating the progression of their skills toward more precise and coherent language use.

Hypothesis 4. Instruction should be responsive to the affective as well as the cognitive needs of students, and their different personalities, preferences, and learning styles should be taken into account.

Hypothesis 5. Cultural understanding must be promoted in various ways so that students are sensitive to other cultures and are prepared to live more harmoniously in the target-language community.

Source: Omaggio Hadley, A. (2001). *Teaching language in context*, p. 90-91.

Hypothesis 1

This activity falls somewhat short of meeting the primary goal of the first hypothesis, which asks that learners do things in the classroom that native speakers of a language would really do. In real life, adults spend very little time pointing at pictures of animals—or even the animals themselves—and naming them. Names of animals do come up while reading a picture book or telling a story, though. Would that be a better way to present the activity to the children? When else do native speakers use animal names?

The condition set out in Corollary 1 of the first hypothesis is not met, because the students are using the teacher's words and pictures rather than their own. It might be more meaningful to the children if they were allowed to create the animal drawings and labels themselves before the group vocabulary activity begins. Corollary 2 is not implemented very well either, because all of the interaction is between the full class and the teacher. Is this perhaps an activity that the children could be taught to run themselves in groups of two or three?

As described, the vocabulary activity does not follow the guidance given in Corollary 3 because it does not encourage students to do anything but repeat words in isolation. They are not asked to add more words of their choosing with a similar theme, nor are they given an opportunity to create even short sentences. One possible solution would be to ask students to partner up at the end of the activity and tell each other, in full sentences, something about three different animals that they saw in the drawings. This follow-up could perhaps be a written activity for children who have basic literacy skills.

To come closer to addressing Corollary 4, the instructor would need to carry out this activity without using any English. However, even if no English is used, the teacher may not sound much like what students would hear if they had a chance to listen in on regular adult speakers talking about animals at home or on the street.

Hypothesis 2

This activity is perhaps of only moderate usefulness according to Hypothesis 2 because, again, adult native speakers of indigenous languages spend very little time reciting names of animals. It is important to ask when animal names would be used. In social songs or blessings? On hunting trips? How could the vocabulary lesson be made more like real settings where people talk about animals?

Hypothesis 3

If the instructor carries out the activity as described above, modeling correct responses after hearing the students' answers, Hypothesis 3 is probably met. There are many ways to correct student responses, but restating the correct answer for the group is perfectly reasonable for this type of activity. If any of the suggestions listed above under Hypothesis 1 were worked into the exercise, however, more thought would need to be put into correction strategies. In general, the more communication-intensive a lesson is, the less overt the corrections should be. In a lesson based on memorizing lists or verb forms, immediate correction is not disruptive. If, on the other hand, two students are asked to engage in a brief conversation about something and they seem to be getting their point across to each other, it is more disruptive to interrupt and correct them on the spot than to make note of errors quietly and bring them up to the full group after the activity is over.

Hypothesis 4

This hypothesis deals with personal learning styles and with the way learning something makes us feel. Different people require different kinds of learning experiences. Some learn by hearing, others by seeing, and others by touching and moving objects. Having students draw their own animals as suggested previously might allow physical and visual learners to get more from the lesson. Being able to select their own favorite animals may also help them feel that they have contributed something important to the group and that their interests are being acknowledged by the instructor. Allowing students to physically move their animal pictures around the room—taping them to a different part of the bulletin board based on the environments where their animal lives (streams, clearings, deep forest, etc.)—could also help meet the needs of different learners.

Hypothesis 5

As it is described, the vocabulary flashcard lesson may not do all that it could to promote cultural awareness. Some of the modifications discussed above bring it closer to meeting the Hypothesis 5 objectives, but it may still be useful not only to present an activity that is in keeping with Native American attitudes toward animals, but to provide students the tools they need to explore the differences that exist between Native practices and Euro-American views. As part of their language curriculum, students should learn how to compare and contrast these cultures, show empathy and objectivity, and seek additional information when confronted with views and practices with which they are not familiar.

Most teachers who use Omaggio Hadley's guidelines appreciate the positive approach that they encourage. Rather than giving a firm list of things that should not be done at all, they provide a set of objectives that curriculum teams can use as they discuss the kinds of activities that their programs should use. Very seldom will a teacher have to abandon a favorite activity completely, because a careful application of these guidelines will help him or her to make simple adaptations that will maximize its educational potential.

Some language instructors may be curious about whether there are methods that really cannot be fixed and therefore ought to be eliminated from consideration. James Lee and Bill VanPatten suggest that ineffective teaching methods are not so much the result of specific classroom methods but of certain mistaken beliefs about language and how it is learned. They offer five examples of mistaken beliefs that contribute to reduced student success.

First, they suggest that many language teachers who received classroom instruction believe that they should teach the way they were taught. However, people who become good at a second language usually have had two things that their own students do not get: extended, immersion-like experiences with the language and a higher than usual desire to learn.[11] Elders or other fluent adult speakers who learned English by memorizing words in a classroom often do not realize just how much English they were hearing and seeing outside the school in books, magazines, television, movies, radio, and so on. Imagine how well the Native American language learners would do if they had all of those things going on in their environment in a traditional language!

Second, many language teachers believe that exercises or drills help students learn the rules of language. Research indicates, however, that only activities that require students to understand and create language based on their own life and interests seem to lead to communicative proficiency.[12] As Warm Springs elder Adeline Miller observes, real progress comes when children in the language program actually use the language:

> *I feel strongly about this teaching, because I think it's wonderful that these teachers ... can take the time and work with children and teach. But I think once they get the basics, then I think they should go into sentences and that's where the learning's going to be. If they could start sentences to*

where the children in the classroom could converse amongst themselves and you could hear it, you're making progress then.

The third mistaken belief is that students need to have grammar rules explained to them. Studies show that although adult and adolescent learners often like to know how things work, lessons in grammar do not help them use the language any better than students who do not get any rules explained to them. The conclusion of researchers is that a certain amount of explaining may help older learners feel more comfortable, but if explaining takes too long, there will be less time to devote to better activities. Young children do not typically require explanations to feel comfortable about learning to say something.[13]

Fourth, there is a tendency to blame all mistakes on the students' first language, while in fact many of the errors seen in the speech and writing of learners comes from other sources.[14] We will discuss the benefits and challenges of working with students who already know a first language in greater detail below.

Finally, Lee and VanPatten suggest that most language teachers believe that students must learn paradigms to communicate in their second language. Paradigms are usually presented as sets of charts or lists that display all of the possible forms a single verb or noun may take. These charts are clearly not necessary, since children all over the world learn their home language without ever seeing a box filled with verb endings.[15]

Lee and VanPatten's observations are consistent with the experience of authors such as Leanne Hinton who have written materials specifically for use in Native American language learning. In her recent language-teaching manual, *How to Keep Your Language Alive*, Hinton reiterates the fact that formal grammar study is not a necessary part of language learning and that translation drills interfere with the learning process. She adds a number of additional observations specific to the teaching of Native American languages. She highlights the importance of speaking (rather than writing) for beginning learners, rejects the suggestion that languages cannot be taught without classrooms, expensive published materials, trained teachers, and strong community support, and reassures adults that language learning can happen at any age.[16]

Research-based principles such as those we have been discussing are invaluable to those involved in the revitalization effort, but drawing on the wisdom and experience of those who have been running language projects is equally important. According to a group of researchers associated with the Santa Fe-based Indigenous Language Institute, successful programs tend to share several features. These include the use of teams, providing opportunities for immersion in the language, being family oriented, setting clear goals, working to produce a few very fluent speakers quickly in order to have teachers to spread around later, balancing tradition with modern approaches, resolving language variation issues, settling political questions, and perseverance.[17]

Measuring Gains in the Classroom

One of the first rules of teaching in a formal educational setting is that the assessment defines the curriculum. No matter what the curriculum planners decide the focus of instruction should be, students will invariably gravitate toward the things that are getting tested the most. If natural, authentic conversational ability is the primary goal of a language program, the tasks that students perform for purposes of receiving a grade must at least imitate aspects of natural, authentic conversation. Teachers who tell their students that the goal of a course is oral proficiency and then proceed to test using nothing but vocabulary lists and other written, fill-in-the-blank exercises will probably be disappointed with their students' conversational ability at the end of the term.

Even in programs that do not require the grading of students, assessment is an important tool for learners, teachers, and program administrators. Adolescent and adult learners in particular seem to have a psychological need for feedback on their performance as learners. Teachers need information about whether the students are achieving mastery of each lesson's objectives. Administrators need evidence that funding and personnel are being utilized appropriately.

There are many types of assessments, and many reasons for giving assessments. For the moment, we will keep in mind just two broad categories. *Formative* assessments are performed in order to provide feedback to students. They are given regularly throughout a course and allow the instructor and students to work together to identify areas of progress and to overcome specific challenges. *Summative* assessments are used less frequently and are typically done for administrative reasons. A good summative assessment will give a snapshot of a student's mastery of specific course objectives and, in the case of language programs housed in a public school, provide a justification for whatever grade is to be registered with the school administration.

Summative assessments can help language programs compare different groups within their program or compare the successes of one program with those of another. Summative assessments should ideally meet requirements for high school graduation or the admissions standards used by Oregon's public universities. However, in order to interface with these external programs, a common, widely accepted measurement of proficiency is needed. Such a measurement exists in the form of the *ACTFL Proficiency Guidelines*, first published in official form in 1986. The guidelines provide descriptions of certain stages of linguistic development in each of the main skill areas recognized at the time: reading, writing, speaking, listening, and culture. Because these guidelines have become so thoroughly embedded in the language-teaching profession, it is important to have a good understanding of how they are constructed and how they may be used.

Under the ACTFL guidelines, students with no functional ability are considered Novice-range learners, and as they acquire skills they work through sub-levels labeled Novice-Low, Novice-Mid, and Novice-High. Once students become capable of creating original language rather than just repeating back lists or memorized responses, they are considered Intermediate students. Again, this broad level is divided into Low, Mid and High. Students who are capable of extended discourse and display excellent accuracy in most tasks may be classified as Advanced-Low, -Mid, or -High. Although the government-produced scale from which the ACTFL guidelines were originally adapted includes equivalents of Superior (approximating the type of language use that is seen in educated native speakers) and even higher levels, ACTFL researchers have concluded that descriptions of those levels are unnecessary because they are seldom reached by second-language learners in standard k-12 and undergraduate college programs.

By far the most developed and most widely used of the proficiency guidelines is the speaking component, which received a major update in 1999. In the years leading up to the publication of the *Guidelines*, ACTFL unveiled a test tied to its oral proficiency descriptions called the Oral Proficiency Interview (OPI).

The OPI has a simple, four-stage design. In the *warm-up* stage, the interviewer asks questions that put the person being examined at ease and help him or her get settled into using the language. In the *level check* stage, the interviewer attempts to find the level (Novice-Mid, Novice-High, etc.) at which the person being examined displays a solid, even performance. At that point, the interviewer enters the *probe* stage, during which the difficulty of the conversation is repeatedly adjusted in order to determine the point at which the student's communicative ability breaks down. For some proficiency levels, this stage requires the use of situation cards that are used for brief role-plays. After the examiner has established the score, there is a *wind-down* stage that returns the conversation to a level that is comfortable for the person being examined so that he or she will leave with a feeling of accomplishment.

The format of the test is simple to explain, but administering a valid OPI is a skill that requires a great deal of practice and expenditure of resources. In order to protect the validity of the test, ACTFL requires that only interviews conducted by trained and certified testers be considered official. Certification is an expensive and time-consuming process that is currently unavailable for Native American languages because there are as yet no ACTFL-approved trainers. But even where certified OPI testers are available, using it as a summative assessment at the end of a program or academic year is a more realistic expectation.

Although ACTFL certification is not possible or perhaps even desirable for Native American languages at this time, language teachers who are working in a formal classroom setting in a public school can learn to use the OPI, OPI-based, or similar proficiency-oriented assessments in their own programs. The Confederation in Oregon for Language Teaching (COFLT) offers workshops for Oregon language teachers who are interested in using an exam called the Oregon Oral Assessment, an interview-based exam that borrows heavily from the ACTFL model. COFLT leaders have expressed a desire to assist Oregon's Native American communities with their revitalization efforts and have some limited tribal representation on their board of directors, but integration of Native languages into the state training and testing program has not progressed very quickly.

Recognizing the limitations of the ACTFL assessment program and its state counterparts, what purpose does it serve to incorporate ACTFL-like proficiency ratings in indigenous-language revitalization programs? Briefly, the ACTFL guidelines were a critical part of the transformation of the language-teaching profession described previously that brought us all closer to meeting the needs of multilingual, multicultural learners. The ACTFL guidelines provided the first workable scale that allowed classroom teachers to measure communicative ability rather than the ability to reproduce vocabulary lists or grammar charts, and the efforts by ACTFL to promote its standards hastened professional acceptance of the proficiency agenda. On a more practical level, the guidelines provide a way for instructors to communicate to learners that oral skills are in fact important and a worthy use of study time. Furthermore, they allow curriculum planners to recognize what level the learners typically reach at the end of an instructional period or academic year and to construct activities at the correct level of complexity for the majority of the group.

Although the details of the published ACTFL descriptions do not perfectly match the interests and values of Native communities in Oregon and elsewhere, the underlying structure provides a solid theoretical base upon which new, more appropriate descriptions can be formulated. Indigenous-language teachers from Oregon have in recent years collaborated with the Northwest Indian Language Institute (NILI) staff at the University of Oregon on a set of ACTFL-like guidelines that are more consistent with the goals and cultural perspectives of Oregon's Native communities.

Proficiency Ratings: Under the Hood

As mentioned above, the specific details of the ACTFL proficiency descriptions often cause confusion and consternation when applied to the indigenous-language recovery setting. However, under the details lie some simple principles that hold true for all languages. This brief dissection of the descriptions may provide some clarity to those who wish to use them as they now exist or participate in future adaptations or revisions at the state or local level.

The official ACTFL proficiency descriptions take into account four specific aspects of language use. The first is the type of real-world *tasks or functions* the learner can expect to be able to carry out. Novice learners are expected to be able to communicate only with memorized formulas such as greetings between friends and family members, but Advanced learners should be able to carry out just about any task within the community, even if there are surprises or complications.

The second aspect of language that plays into a proficiency rating is the *context* in which the learner can operate. Novice learners will only be able to function in very common informal settings and communicate about a highly restricted number of topics (self, family), while Advanced learners will be able to operate in formal settings (like giving a speech to a group) and deal with a much broader array of topics.

The third component of a proficiency rating is *accuracy*, or how well the learner can understand or be understood by native speakers. Novice speakers will probably make too many mistakes to be understood by fluent elders who are not used to working with language learners and sometimes even by the language teachers, but Advanced speakers should be able to communicate accurately enough that their errors will not confuse or annoy any fluent speaker in the community.

The final part of the equation is *text type*, or the complexity of the language the student can produce. Please note that "text" in this case is a linguistics term that refers to any form of linguistic production, whether it be written, oral, or even using signs or gestures. Novice learners may only produce lists, such as in our hypothetical animal flashcard activity, while Advanced learners will typically communicate in complete paragraphs with a clear logical structure that ties them together.

Even if a revitalization program does not wish to use ACTFL-type assessments, the guidelines provide a clear picture of what kinds of expectations teachers should have at each stage of their learners' development. Careful attention to the ACTFL descriptions will allow teachers and curriculum planners to construct lessons that challenge learners but do not require skills they are not yet ready to handle.

So how long does it take to move from Novice to complete fluency? One thing we know is that progress is faster at the beginning of the proficiency scale than at the end; students will move much more quickly through the Novice range than they will through the Intermediate range. According to research done by the Foreign Service Institute and reported in the 1982 *ETS Oral Proficiency Testing Manual*, the length of time it takes medium-aptitude learners to reach the equivalent of an ACTFL Advanced rating in speaking can be considerable. For languages that share a lot of structure and vocabulary with English (Spanish, French, German, etc.), it took at least 480 contact hours with the language instructor to reach the Advanced level. For languages that are structurally very different from English—and Oregon's indigenous languages would undoubtedly fit into this category—it took at least 1,320 hours. For Native American language programs that are allowed only thirty minutes of contact time a week in a public school, these numbers are sobering. In an entire thirty-five-week school year, students might receive just eighteen and a half contact hours with their language teachers. At that pace, we could expect Advanced-level fluency in just over seventy-one years!

Formative Assessments

Recognizing that OPIs are best suited for the occasional summative assessment and for major curriculum planning, how should instructors go about collecting information about the daily progress of their students in each of the main skill areas?

Many language-testing experts now agree that working assessment opportunities into the everyday classroom routine is the best way to go. This does not mean that there has to be a test every time the class meets. It means that the instructor should construct all classroom activities in such a way that the learners get some kind of feedback on their linguistic performance. That feedback may be formal or casual, recorded in a grade book or not, and may often come from a peer rather than the teacher.

Ideally, daily assessment activities would follow Omaggio Hadley's guidelines: they would copy the kinds of language and situations native speakers would really find outside the classroom, allow students to do lots of different things with language (narrate, describe, convince, etc.), promote accuracy without making grammatical precision the only measurement of success in the activity, respond to the needs of different types of learners, and require attention to cultural issues.

In order to help language teachers more fully incorporate the principles expressed in *Standards for Foreign Language Learning* into their everyday practice, ACTFL has published guidelines for an assessment model for classroom use known as the Integrated Performance Assessment (IPA). The IPA is a project-based model that allows learners to engage in exploration of a culturally significant topic while practicing interpersonal, interpretive, and presentational skills in both writing and speech. ACTFL's *Integrated Performance Assessment Manual*[18] presents examples that are suitable for any proficiency level. Schools are often criticized for "teaching to the test," but when the test models real-world skills that language learners need, there should be no cause for complaints.

Language Acquisition

With very few exceptions, students in Native American language programs in Oregon are native speakers of English who are learning a traditional language of their community as a second language. As a rule, the language learned at home—usually English—will continue to be a learner's dominant language. This does not mean that language programs cannot turn out fluent speakers. However, just how fluent the students are likely to become depends on several factors, not all of which are under the direct control of program coordinators. These include the age and motivation of the students, the type of instruction delivered, and the community's attitudes toward traditional languages. Even if all of these factors line up in the students' favor, what we know about the natural variation of language suggests that the final product may not turn out exactly as expected by program planners.

First and Second Languages

Nearly all children are successful at learning a first language, and they seem to do it with very little effort. Regardless of the language spoken in the home, the learning process tends to follow a fairly predictable schedule. Studies show that by four months of age babies can tell the difference between the sounds of their own home language and those of other languages, even when spoken by the same voice.[19] The first simple words appear at about one year of age, two-word sentences at eighteen months, and the first use of structures like verb suffixes at about two years. By age four, most children will have a basic mastery of their home language and a vocabulary of up to sixteen hundred words.[20] People really never stop learning their first language; as we are exposed to new situations, people, and ideas, we learn new words and discover more ways to communicate with others.

Second-language learners, unlike babies, don't begin at zero. Whether they begin their exposure to a second language as school-aged children or adults, they arrive with a certain understanding of how language works. The second-language learner will typically apply this understanding to the new language without really noticing that it is happening. Despite this apparent head start, second-language learners are not as universally successful as first-language learners, and the effort required seems to increase with age.

One significant barrier for second-language learners is that some of the rules that people acquire as they learn their first language are universal principles that transfer well, and others do not transfer well at all. For example, infants must discover, albeit subconsciously, that the sounds of language include vowels and consonants before they can understand and produce language. That knowledge is useful in learning any language. However, different languages use different sets of vowels and consonants. If a student cannot learn to distinguish between the sounds of his or her first language and those of the target language, communication errors will result. This inappropriate application of the rules and parameters of a first language to the target language is known as negative transference.

Language-acquisition experts such as James Lee and Bill VanPatten have asserted that negative transference is not as significant a problem as previously thought.[21] What must be kept in mind with indigenous languages in the United States, however, is that the pressure of English is much greater here than in the countries of origin of more commonly taught languages such as Spanish or French. Not only are individual learners in revitalization programs already programmed for English by the time they reach school age, but the traditional languages themselves have been subjected to strong English influence for over one hundred fifty years. This exposure has resulted in some profound linguistic changes—new words based on English roots, for example. More significantly, the adoption of English as the primary language of everyday life on Oregon's reservations has made it impossible for learners of indigenous languages to be immersed in authentic traditional language the way students of Spanish are when they study abroad in Spain or Mexico. There is no geographic space anywhere in the world where one can experience Oregon's indigenous languages and cultures as they existed before European contact. We'll spend a bit more time examining both the linguistic and social dimensions of English language contact.

Linguistic Interference

A famous example of this type of negative transfer—also known as *interference*—comes from the period of time when native Hawai'ian speakers were learning English as a second language. The Hawai'ian sound system is different from that of English in several significant ways. First, Hawai'ian has only about half as many vowel sounds as English. Second, Hawai'ian is missing some of the most common consonants of English, like /r/ and /s/. Third, Hawai'ian does not allow words to end in a consonant, nor does it allow two consonants in a row. When early Hawai'ian learners of English applied their own language's pronunciation rules to their new language, the results were sometimes barely recognizable. Some of these forms still exist in popular Hawai'ian speech and are perceived by the public as being actual Hawai'ian words even though they come from English. The holiday song that wishes us a "melekalikamaka," is actually just saying "Merry Christmas" using Hawai'ian sound rules.

As we see in Figure 5.6, "melekalikamaka" is the result of what happens when English sounds are replaced with Hawai'ian ones. English vowels are changed to the closest-sounding Hawai'ian

mɛɹik ɹɪs mʌs
| | | | | | | | | | | |
melikalikamaka

Figure 5.6 Source: Akmajian, A. et al. (2001). *Linguistics.*

vowels. Where English has an /r/, Hawai'ian uses /l/. Where English has an /s/, Hawai'ian uses /k/. All consonant clusters in English are broken up in Hawai'ian by adding an extra /a/ sound. Finally, all words that have a consonant at the end in English have an /a/ added to them in Hawai'ian:

Interference can occur not only with the sounds of language, but with word structures (morphology) and sentence structures (syntax) as well.

An example of a potential problem at the morphological level is the difference between the way English uses nouns and the way Oregon native languages use them. In English, nouns are quite simple words that do not allow very many suffixes or carry a lot of grammatical information. English speakers depend on word order to communicate which noun in a sentence is doing what job. That's why the sentence "Man bites dog" does not have the same meaning as "Dog bites man," even though both have exactly the same words. Moving the nouns *dog* and *man* from their original spaces changes everything.

But the mismatch between English and other world languages goes even deeper. A noun like dog, for example, may have an -*s* added to the end to indicate that there is more than one animal present. It may also have an - 's added to show that something belongs to the dog-"the dog's collar." That is all that modern English nouns can really do, and English-speaking children start out expecting that nouns in their new language will allow those same two bits of information—plural -*s* and possession - 's—to be shown in the same way.

As it turns out, indigenous languages in Oregon don't have plurals ending in -*s* or possession ending in - 's. To further complicate issues for the English speaker, most Oregon languages have other grammatical relationships that English does not even recognize. Languages from the Sahaptian family even embed nouns within the verb of a sentence rather than treat them as separate words.[23]

There are huge differences between the verb system of English and those of Oregon's indigenous languages as well. English requires the use of a pronoun (*I, you, he* ...) with its verbs. The pronoun and verb form together tell the English speaker how many people are doing the action, what gender they are, and when the action is happening. Languages like Klamath, however, don't include any of that kind of information. They can, however, express ideas like the location of an action, direction of an action, or the size and shape of the things being acted upon in the verb itself rather than relying on extra words like English would.

There is also potential for linguistic interference from English at the syntax or word order level. As mentioned above, the fact that English does not allow many grammatical properties to be encoded in the words themselves requires that English speakers stick to a certain word order. Specifically, simple declarative English sentences require that the subject come first, then the verb, and finally the object being acted upon. Languages that use this pattern for their sentences are known as SVO languages. By the time most second-language learners of native Oregon languages reach the classroom, they have already stored away the English SVO pattern in their subconscious and are very likely to attempt to apply that word order to any subsequent language they come in contact with. However, because most indigenous Oregon languages encode a more complex set of grammatical relationships in each word, they do not require the rigid word order of English. Learners who assume that the subject always comes first may frequently misinterpret what native speakers are saying. Another example of a word order problem is the use of prepositions, which in English come before the noun they're associated with: *before* dinner, *under* the table. Languages such as Tolowa put that kind of information after the noun.[24]

Not only do sounds and structures get copied from one language to another, but meanings as well. Languages in contact with each other often create *calques*, which are literal translations of a concept in the first language that doesn't always make complete sense in the second. Language learners are particularly adept at making up new words in the language they are learning, based on concepts that exist in English. This invention of words can become a group phenomenon, especially when a large number of second-language learners share the same first language. What often happens as students spend increasingly more time together is the development of a special classroom hybrid or *interlanguage* that mixes features of English into the second language. The members of the group communicate very effectively with each other using this classroom code, but native speakers from the outside may not understand them.

Language teachers often become frustrated by the many errors their students make while learning a new language skill. The frustration quickly spreads to the students, creating a negative atmosphere and inhibiting students from taking the kinds of risks that language learning requires. Language experts have long recognized that in order for language acquisition to happen, the classroom must always feel like a safe and welcoming environment in which the natural trial-and-error process of language learning can take place.[25] Knowing the source of student errors helps instructors be objective and supportive as the learners develop greater accuracy over time.

Cultural Interference

We have seen the many ways that a learner's contact with English can interfere with acquisition of a traditional language. Of much greater concern in terms of the overall prospects for success in a language program, however, is the degree to which English has displaced the use of traditional languages in daily life.

One of the more important concepts of sociolinguistics is that of the *domain,* or specific time and place where language use may be found. The home, workplace, church, or school could each be thought of as separate domains. With the arrival of English-speaking Euro-American colonizers, parallel systems of domains emerged in the same geographical space. Although in theory it is possible for two language communities in contact with each other to retain all of their domains, the nearly universal outcome historically has been the spread of one language at the expense of the other. The language that wins over speakers from the other is typically the language that is most associated with economic and social power. The shift usually begins in social institutions controlled by the more socially prestigious group—schools and government, for example—and then spreads to more intimate domains as the marginalized group begins to internalize the new power structure and even buys into any negative and racist attitudes held by the group in control. Once the home domain is claimed by the outside language, traditional language learning in the home stops and the language is well on its way to extinction.

In most of Oregon's Native communities, the takeover of domains by English is nearly complete. Whether at church, in school, at a government office, or at home, English is the preferred language among most Indians. The number of spaces where English seems out of place is increasingly limited and often considered so intimate or sacred that typical members of the community are seldom exposed to them.

It is easy to assume that the loss of traditional languages is a direct result of anti-Indian policies carried out by the U.S. government. However, even language-diversity advocates point out that the reasons for the displacement of Indian languages in public spaces are far more complex and that, to a certain extent, they reflect the way tribal members have chosen to respond to the difficult social and economic circumstances created by the government's efforts at cultural genocide.

James Crawford[26] suggests that the loss of language domains can be tied to factors such as migration out of the reservation, a feeling that only English allows for employment in the mainstream economy, a preference for mass media over traditional storytelling and other pastimes, and the selection of non-Indian role models by the younger generations. In addition, he observes that non-Native values such as individualism, pragmatism, and materialism have taken root in Native American communities and further eroded the commitment to traditional language and culture. The logical conclusion of these observations, according to Crawford, is that a return to traditional language must also involve a choice: a decision by tribal members to restructure community values in a way that is compatible with traditional language and culture. This conclusion is supported by sociolinguist and revitalization scholar Joshua Fishman, who observes that reversing language shift "is, essentially, a societal reform effort."[27]

Language Variation and Change

A final area of linguistics that has a direct impact on language-revitalization programs is the study of language variation and change. One of the difficulties language teachers encounter is the expectation by fluent adult speakers and elders that heritage-language learners will end up with a style of language just like their own. Any deviation from that model may be considered corrupt or disrespectful. Researchers from the Indigenous Language Institute describe the problem as follows:

> When such activities attempting to reverse language shift occur, oftentimes the "heart of the people" (the language) becomes objectified. Objectified, it is no longer a living, dynamic means of expressing emotions, maintaining intimate relationships, and projecting a unique world. Instead, it becomes a language of study.[28]

What linguistics research offers is the understanding that language variation and change are the mark of a living, thriving language. In healthy languages, differences always exist between the speech patterns of one group or another, and the way people talk changes over time.

There are three primary dimensions of language change. The type of change that occurs across time is known as *diachronic variation*. All aspects of language—the sound system, morphology, and syntax —are subject to change over time. An example is the English word *meat*, which at the time of Shakespeare referred to any type of food, not just the flesh of an animal. Diachronic variation does not seem to take place at a predictable rate. Some aspects of a language may stay the same for hundreds of years, then suddenly undergo a complete upheaval. Although it's difficult to predict when large changes will occur, we are currently in a period of time when rapid changes in society make it very likely that, at a minimum, traditional languages will need some new words in order to allow speakers to talk about computers, cell phones, and other technological innovations.

Diatopic variation is the difference we can observe between groups of people who live in different geographical areas of a single, larger language community. When people talk about dialects, they are usually referring to these different regional styles of language use. Again, this type of variation can show up in pronunciation, word forms, or word order. In most cases, speakers from one dialect region are able to understand most of what people from another dialect region are saying. In politically complex communities, people from one dialect may choose to see themselves as speakers of a completely different language even though the structure and vocabulary of the dialects involved are very similar, or they may emphasize differences in vocabulary or pronunciation to help maintain a separate community identity. An example of regional variation from English is the word used to refer to sandwiches. What people in Oregon might call a *sub* is called a *hoagie* or a *grinder* in other parts of the country. To a certain extent, regional variation is connected to the historical origin of members of a community (who may have migrated from another area) or perhaps to isolation in an ecological zone that is different from that of other speakers.

Perhaps the most complex type of variation is the difference observed between members of different social groupings who live in the same language community. This is sometimes referred to as *diastratic variation*. The reason this type of variation is so complex is that each person in a language community has many different aspects to their identity. Any one of those identities can be associated with a particular style of language use, and we switch between each of these styles many times during a single day as we encounter different people from diverse social groups.

A simple example of social variation is the use of slang by young people. Linguistically speaking, slang is just as sophisticated as any other kind of language. What is important about it is that it is used to help teenagers establish a bond with other people their age and to assert their growing sense of independence from their parents. As

Linn and her colleagues observe, in some indigenous communities there may be styles of language associated with certain families, clans, bands, genders, and ages as well.[29] One of the challenges that heritage-language programs face is the need to determine ahead of time what styles of language need to be offered in order to make sure that learners are exposed to all the styles they will need to fit the most important facets of their identity.

Perhaps the type of socially linked variation that causes the most consternation in Native American language programs is the students' use of a mixture of both English and their heritage language in the same sentence. The jumbling of words from different languages leaves teachers with the impression that the students are not applying themselves or that they are treating the traditional language with disrespect.

There are certainly cases where beginning students throw in an English word or phrase after becoming frustrated at not being able to formulate what they want to say comfortably in their heritage language. A patient and experienced teacher will be able to help these students manage their anxiety and find a communication strategy that will allow them to stay in the target language. However, when proficient students or naturally bilingual community members use sentences that contain grammatical elements from both English and the traditional language, something very different is taking place. Rather than being simply a symptom of incomplete acquisition of one language or the other, this *code mixing* is, at least in part, being used as a social marker for a group of people who see bilingualism or biculturalism as a key aspect of their identity. The mixing of languages stands as a symbolic statement that these people share a reality that is not fully understood either by monolingual English speakers or by monolingual speakers of an indigenous language. The need to create a sense of solidarity with a social group is very strong, so efforts by language programs or teachers to eradicate code mixing from a whole community of bilingual speakers are unlikely to succeed.

Regardless of the decisions that are made about what styles of language should be put into the curriculum, it is fundamentally important to remember that the learners themselves may make different choices than their teachers about how to use the language as they become more confident. As language-change expert Jean Aitchison observes:

> the puristic attitude toward language—the idea that there
> is an absolute standard of correctness which should be

maintained—has its origin in a natural nostalgic tendency, supplemented and intensified by social pressures .... Purists behave as if there was a vintage year when language achieved a measure of excellence which we should all strive to maintain. In fact, there never was such a year.[30]

If traditional languages are to survive, language teachers must be prepared to accept and encourage this kind of linguistic experimentation. It is a sign that they are succeeding in bringing their language back to life.

Conclusion

Although there has been a justifiable reluctance among teachers in Native communities to get bogged down in university research or to construct programs to meet the expectations of non-Indian experts in the areas of language and education, the language-teaching profession has probably never been better equipped to provide the training and resources needed by indigenous people involved in revitalization programs. The recently adopted National Standards provide a clear starting point for curriculum development and a common language for educators and program administrators. More importantly, they do so in a way that invites community involvement in their local implementation. The language-teaching profession's new-found appreciation for teaching language in a real-world context provides better tools for heritage learners than previous educational models because it recognizes the inseparability of language and culture. Language theory helps identify some of the difficulties inherent in teaching a traditional language in an environment that is dominated by English. An understanding of the principles of language variation and change help teachers and community members understand that successful revitalization will never look like a snapshot of the past, but that it will take on new shapes and sounds as the community moves into the future.

Conclusion

Now is the time to assist Oregon Natives in revitalizing their languages. Since beginning work on this book, we have lost more elders who had helped keep the languages alive. There are tribal members all over the state who have devoted much of their time and energy to breathing life back into Oregon Native languages, but they need the support of the wider community. School administrators and teachers must learn what it means to revitalize a language and they should provide stepping stones, rather than road blocks. Tribal councils need to understand the importance that language revitalization holds for many of their members. Language renewal and self-respect often go hand in hand. Universities should publicize the fact that Native language study fulfills the requirement to study another language as much as any of the standard European languages that are commonly taught. In addition, universities should institute programs that will help train the next generation of Native language teachers. A steady source of funding for Native language programs would be very useful, but financial resources are actually less important than human resources. At the center lie the people whom we interviewed for this project, people who spend their energy healing the ties of broken linguistic transmission. Their job can be made easier if Oregonians of all cultures express our support for the revitalization of Oregon's first languages. In so doing we show our respect for the various cultures who cared for this land for countless generations.

Natives and immigrants alike should be aware of the colonial history of genocide and oppression that has influenced conditions today. The Native population of the state was decimated by new diseases. The survivors were deprived of their land and forced together on reservations. Christian missionaries and the U.S. government attempted to wipe out Native cultures by denigrating Indian ways while implementing a dominant foreign culture. In the process, Indian people were marginalized and discriminated against. Their languages were thought to tie them too closely to their earlier way of life and so the very way they spoke was targeted for destruction. Through the separation of children from their parents and grandparents, cultural transmission was disrupted and many of their stories were no longer told.

The way that we think about language has a tremendous influence on which and how many languages we learn. Elders still living today can attest to the multilingual Native past. Over time, this

147

multilingualism morphed into English monolingualism, helped along by a variety of policies and other political moves. Since 1990, policies that support the teaching of Native languages have been passed, but not without resistance from a growing movement to support English as the official language of the country. We would never argue against the necessity of knowing English in this country, but English hardly needs legislative support. What we have seen is that legislative support of English usually means the withdrawal of support from all other languages that actually need it. This manner of thinking views languages as competing with each other, rather than supporting each other and contributing to expanded mental capacity and cross-cultural understanding.

We need to honor those individuals and families who continued speaking their languages and generously shared them with researchers in the past and with students today. Scientific interest in Native languages and cultures produced a written record, but researchers did not focus on the perpetuation of these languages and cultures, only their documentation. These documents must be read within the context of their collection, that of salvage linguistics. Many tribal language activists today find this documentation to be useful, others feel marginalized by the arcane scientific vocabulary that further distances them from the language of their ancestors. Tribal language programs have been working hard to record elders and create documentation for future generations, but the task of archiving these materials for easy access overwhelms many. An answer may lie in the digitalization of records. This holds promise for a more equal dissemination of material that for generations has been tucked away in archives far from where the data were collected and far from the people who have a personal interest in using these languages.

Very young children do not have to be taught a language; they simply learn what they hear spoken regularly around them. This is why pre-school immersion has been so successful in language-revitalization programs around the world. Children's linguistic apprenticeship cannot stop, however, when they enter public school. As easily as languages are learned at that young age, they can be forgotten. Learning a language requires sustained effort over many years, so we must build into our language programs interesting curricula that grow with the children. For successful revitalization, young people must adopt the language as their own. This means that they will likely introduce changes, since language is completely integrated into culture and cultures are dynamic, not static. Some of these changes elders may dislike. Nonetheless, we must remember that languages are bundles of varieties, each one rooted in real-world situations, and language teaching should center on communication in a variety of contexts. The rules of language use vary from culture to culture and from situation to situation and even from generation to generation. The aim of language teaching should be communicative competence.

Speaking a language does not mean that one automatically knows how to teach it. Luckily, Oregon Native language teachers have worked hard at learning new skills. They have attended classes at the American Indian Language Development Institute in Tucson, Arizona, the Piegan Institute in Browning, Montana, and at the Northwest Indian Language Institute in Eugene, Oregon. They have visited long-standing language-revitalization programs in Hawaii and consulted with the leaders of the Language Nest program in New Zealand. They belong to listserves and meet with one another to exchange ideas. They have a difficult job because they feel as if they have to do everything at once: improve their own language skills, learn teaching strategies, decide on which orthographic system to use, develop curricula for all the different age groups, and most importantly, teach. All of this is in addition to being good role models for their students by participating in tribal events and fulfilling family obligations.

This is a time for us to band together to promote the value of multilingualism in our society and the deep respect for cultural diversity that it brings. We need to honor the culture and language bearers of the original inhabitants of our state, both those who grew up in a Native language and those who continue to work so hard to learn Oregon Native languages so that they can pass them on to others. Passing on the language also means passing on stories, songs, prayers, poems, jokes, and many other forms of verbal art. These encapsulate culture and make younger generations want to participate in its richness. Some of these pieces of encapsulated culture will tell us about traditional subsistence activities and alternative ways of seeing the universe that may be helpful in our post-industrial society. Learning about cultures and cultural contact in our country from multiple points of view should be an important element of everyone's education that can help people understand the state of relations today and better inform our actions in the future. Educating a population that is more sensitive to issues of language and culture paves the way for a stronger democracy.

Appendix: Primary Repositories for Oregon Native American Language Materials

Researchers and Dates	Oregon Languages Studied
American Philosophical Society, 105 South Fifth St., Philadelphia, PA 19106	
Jaime de Angulo 1887-1950	Chinook Jargon, Atfalatin (Tfalati), and
Franz Boas 1858-1942	Chinook Jargon, Clatsop Chinook, Molala, Shasta, Tillamook, Wasco
Roland Dixon 1875-1934	Shasta
Walter Dyk 1899-1972	Wasco, Wishram
Livingston Farrand 1867-1939	Nez Perce
Leo Frachtenberg 1883-1930	Alsea, Coos, Kalapuya, Molala, Siuslaw
Lucy Freeland 1948-1972	Yamhalla dialects of Kalapuya, Knomihu, Shasta, Tualatin
Dell Hymes 1927-	Chinook Jargon, Kalapuya, Siuslaw, Upper Chinook
Melville Jacobs 1902-1971	Chasta Costa, Clackamas, Molala, Santiam Kalapuya, Shasta, Tillamook, Yonkalla
May Mandelbaum 1909-1964	Tillamook
Archie Phinney c.1903-1949	Nez Perce, Sahaptin
Bruce Rigsby c.1930-	Molale, Umatilla, Walla Walla, Yakima
Edward Sapir 1884-1939	Alsea, Chasta Costa, Chinook Jargon, Coos, Takelma, Wasco, Wishram
Morris Swadesh 1909-1967	Nez Perce, Sahaptin
University of California, Berkeley Bancroft Library, Berkeley, CA 94720	
Cora Du Bois 1904-1991	Athabaskan, Chetco, Clackamas, Coos, Galice Creek, Tillamook, Tolowa, Tututni, Upper Coquille
Alfred Kroeber 1876-1960	Athabaskan
Leslie Spier 1893-1961	Modoc, Klamath

University of California, Berkeley, Language Center, B-40 Dwinelle Hall # 2640, Berkeley, CA 94720 (*Audio material with collection dates*)
http://www.mip.berkeley.edu/blc/la

Anonymous n.d.	Northern Paiute
Haruo Aoki 1959	Nez Perce
Phillip M.A.R. Barker 1955 (spoken by Mrs. Grover Pompey et. al)	Klamath
Jane O.Bright 1962	Tolowa

Researchers and Dates	Oregon Languages Studied
William Bright 1950 (spoken by Sargent Sambo)	Shasta
Victor Golla 1962 (spoken by Ida Bensell)	Tututni
Harry Hoijer 1956	Tolowa
Harry Hoijer 1956	Galice
Alfred Kroeber (spoken by Capt. Numana Gilbert Natchez), early 1900s	Northern Paiute
Sven Liljebled n.d.	Nez Perce
Shirley Silver 1957	Shasta
Zoa Swayne n.d.	Nez Perce
Russell Ultan 1964 (spoken by Martha Johnson)	Coos
Deward Walker 1960	Nez Perce
Mary Woodward n.d.	Tolowa

University of Idaho Library, P.O Box 442350, Moscow, ID 83844

Rev. Joseph Mary Cataldo 1837-1928	Nez Perce
Sue L. McBeth 1830-1893	Nez Perce
Anthony Morvillo 1839-1919	Nez Perce
Stephen D. Shawley (late 20th century)	Nez Perce
Mari Watters 1934-1992	Nez Perce

Library of Congress, 101 Independence Ave. SE, Washington, DC 20540

John Peabody Harrington 1884-1961	Alsea, Athabaskan, Chehalis, Chinook, Chinook Jargon, Coos (Hanis and Miluk), Cowlitz, Galice/Applegate, Lower Umpqua, Shasta, Siuslaw, Takelma, Tillamook

The American Folklife Center at the Library of Congress, Archive of Folk Culture (*Audio material with collection dates*)

Samuel Barrett 1907 (sung by Charlie Cowen)	Klamath
Laura Boulton 1946, 1947	Nez Perce, Umatilla, Warm Springs, Yakima
Frachtenburg 1915-16 (Tututni sung by Hoxie Simmons)	Kalapuya, Shasta, Tututni, Upper Umpqua
Melville Jacobs 1929-30 (spoken and sung by Victoria Howard)	Clackamas Chinook, Lakmiyuk, Mary's River, Shasta, Tualatin, Yamhill, Yonkalla
Willard Rhodes, summer 1947	Nez Perce, Wasco

National Anthropological Archives, Smithsonian Institution Museum, 4210 Silver Hill Rd., Suitland, MD 20746

Homer G. Barnett 1906-1985	Chetco, Coos, Galice Creek, Siuslaw, Sixes River, Tillamook, Tututni
Franz Boas 1858-1942	Chinook, Clatsop, Salish, Tillamook
James O. Dorsey 1848-1895	Alsea, Athabaskan, Klikitat, Lower Umpqua, Miluk, Shasta, Siuslaw, Takelma, Yaquina
Philip Drucker 1911-1982	Alsea, Chetco, Clackamas, Hanis, Molala, Lower Umpqua, Takelma, Tillamook, Tututni, Upper Coquille, Upper Umpqua
Livingston Farrand 1867-1939	Alsea, Joshua, Siuslaw, Tututni
Leo J. Frachtenberg 1883-1930	Alsea, Athabaskan, Coos, Hanis, Kalapuya, Lower Umpqua, Molala, Shasta, Siletz Tillamook, Siuslaw
Albert Gatschet 1832-1907	Ahantchuyuk, Chinook Jargon, Clackamas, Klamath, Luckiamute, Modoc, Molala, Nestucca, Tillamook, Tualatin, Upper Umpqua, Yamhill
John Peabody Harrington 1884-1961	Alsea, Athabaskan, Chehalis, Chinook, Chinook Jargon, Coos (Hanis and Miluk), Cowlitz, Galice/Applegate, Lower Umpqua, Shasta, Siuslaw, Takelma, Tillamook
Harry Hull St. Clair 1879-1953	Coos, Takelma, Shoshone
Edward Sapir 1884-1939	Alsea, Chasta Costa, Chinook, Takelma, Wasco, Wishram

University of Nevada, Reno, Library, 1664 N. Virginia St., Reno, Nevada 89557

Warren D'Azevedo 1920-	Paiute
Sven Liljeblad 1899-2000	Paiute, Shoshone
Tim Thornes 1961- (oral interviews recorded 1995-1996)	N. Paiute
Margaret Wheat 1908-1988	Paiute

University of Oregon, 1501 Kincaid St., Eugene, OR 97403

Homer G. Barnett 1906-1985	Chetco, Coos, Galice Creek, Siuslaw, Sixes River, Tillamook, Tututni
Theodore Stern 1917-2005	Klamath, Umatilla (Sahaptin)

Santa Barbara Museum of Natural History, 2559 Puesta Del Sol, Santa Barbara, CA 93105

John Peabody Harrington 1884-1961	Alsea, Athabaskan, Chehalis, Chinook, Chinook Jargon, Coos (Hanis and Miluk), Cowlitz, Galice/Applegate, Lower Umpqua, Shasta, Siuslaw, Takelma, Tillamook

Researchers and Dates	*Oregon Languages Studied*

University of Washington Library, Box 352900, Seattle, WA 98195

Franz Boas 1858-1942	Chinook, Clatsop, Salish, Tillamook
Elizabeth Derr Jacobs 1903-1983	Nehalem Tillamook
Melville Jacobs 1902-1971	Chasta Costa, Clackamas, Molala, Santiam Kalapuya, Shasta, Tillamook, Yonkalla
Mari Watters 1934-1992	Nez Perce

Washington State University Library, Pullman, WA 99164

James M. Cornelison (early 20th century)	Nez Perce
Judy Jones 1960-	Nez Perce
Susan Law McBeth 1830-1893	Nez Perce
Lucullus Virgil McWhorter 1848-1945	Nez Perce, Yakima
Asa Bowen Smith 1809-1886	Nez Perce

Confederated Tribes of Warm Springs, 1233 Veterans St., Warm Springs, OR 97761

Kathryn French 1922-2006	Wasco-Wishram
David French 1918-1994	Wasco-Wishram

Notes

Introduction (pages 1-6)

1. Conklin and Lourie 1983:23.
2. Ibid., 199-200.
3. Ibid., 66-67.
4. Mechelli 2004:757.

Chapter One (pages 7-34)

Notes to map on page 9:
Northern Paiute: Wa-dihtchi-tika,
Hu-nipwi-tika, Pa-tihichi-tika,
Walpapi, Wada-tika, Agai-tika,
Yapa-tika, Gidi-tika (Gidu-Tikadu),
Gwi-nidi-ba
Clatskanie, Tututni: Yukichetunne
(1), Tututne (2), Mikonotunne
(3), Chemetunne (4), Chetleshin
(5), Kwaishtunnetunne (6),
Taltushtentede (Galice) (7),
Kwatami, Upper Coquille, Upper
Umpqua, Shasta Costa, Chetco,
Tolowa, Dakubetede
Lower Chinookan: Clatsop,
Cathlamet
Kiksht: Multnomah, Clackamas,
Cascades, Wasco
Takelman-Kalapuyan: Tualatan,
Kalapooia, Yoncalla, Takelma,
Upland Takelma, Cow Creek
Sahaptin: Tenino, Tygh, Wyam, John
Day, Umatilla

1. Hymes 2007.
2. Boas Collection, Melville Jacobs
   correspondence, July 16, 1926.
   American Philosophical Society
3. Ibid., December 1928.
4. Ibid., July 22, 1933.
5. Aoki 1975.
6. Boas Collection, Melville Jacobs
   correspondence, January 8, 1934.
   American Philosophical Society.
7. Hymes 2007.
8. Samarin 1996:330.
9. Gibbs 1863:preface.
10. U.S. Congress 1863:202.
11. Hendricks 1937:35.
12. Reddick and Collins 2005:5.
13. Thanks to David Lewis for this
    information.
14. Reddick and Collins 2005:8.
15. Gibbs 1863: 1.
16. Op. cit.
17. See Hajda, Zenk, and Boyd 1988;
    Thomason 1983; and Hymes1980.
18. Cash Cash 2005.
19. Schenk 1932:47,9 as cited in
    Samarin 1996:330.
20. Hale 1890:19-20.
21. Boas Collection, Melville Jacobs
    correspondence, February 27, 1933.
    American Philosophical Society.
22. Boyd 1999:29.
23. William Clark, April 3, 1806
    quoted in Boyd 1999:29; and
    Merriwether Lewis, February 7,
    1806 quoted in Boyd 1999:40.
24. Boyd 1999:79-80.
25. Ibid.,134-135.
26. Ibid., 74-75.
27. Ibid., 84
28. Ibid., 94
29. Ibid., 99
30. Ibid., 241, 242
31. Ibid., 143
32. Ibid., 159
33. Second-class citizenship in
    healthcare continued to be an
    issue on reservations. Letters from
    Indians complaining that medicines
    at the reservation were at least
    twenty years old and ineffective are
    included in the SWORP collection.
    The Indians had to raise money
    and leave the reservation to get
    medicines for their illnesses (Lewis
    2002:63).
34. Boyd 1999:164.
35. Boas Collection, Leo Frachtenburg
    correspondence, July 26, 1913.
    American Philosophical Society.
36. Boyd 1999:232.
37. Ibid., 258.
38. Ibid., 247-53.
39. Hymes in Boyd 1999:59.
40. Boyd 1999:97.
41. Jackson 1993:383.
42. Ibid., 451-55.
43. Hall 1978: 30.
44. Confederated Tribes of the Siletz
    Indians of Oregon 1984:10-11.
45. Southwest Oregon Research
    Project Collection, Lindsay
    Applegate, Box 4, Folder 12.
    University of Oregon.
46. Kip 1855.
47. Hudson 1993:30.

48. Dominica 1959:145.
49. Ibid., 52.
50. Ibid., 73.
51. Report of Indian Peace Commissioners 1868, 16-17, quoted in Reyhner and Eder 2004:74.
52. Jackson 1993:451-54.
53. U.S. Congress 1859.
54. Southwest Oregon Research Project Collection, 268, Series 2, Box, 2, folder 1. University of Oregon.
55. Ibid., Box 5, folder 3.
56. Harrison 1887:115.
57. Ibid., 147.
58. Southwest Oregon Research Project Collection, 268 Series 2, Box 5, folder 12. University of Oregon.
59. U.S. Congress 1863.
60. Southwest Oregon Research Project Collection, 268, series 2, Box 5, folder 2. University of Oregon.
61. Carney 1999:70.
62. See letters by J. Minthorn, June 2, 1884, and P. K. Sinnott in Southwest Oregon Research Project Collection 268, series 2, Box 3, folder 5. University of Oregon.
63. Lemmon 1941:26.
64. Ryan 1931.
65. Ironically, this former boarding school now houses the Warm Springs Language Program.
66. Bonnell 1997:94.
67. Reyhner and Eder 2004:177.

Chapter Two (pages 35-68)

1. At the height of cultural disruption in the nineteenth century, new Native religions formed in response to forced acculturation. The Ghost Dance originated with the Paiute prophet Wodziwob in 1869 and spread throughout Oregon, Nevada, and California. It was followed twenty years later by an even more expansive Ghost Dance movement. These religious movements were based on the belief that, if sacred dances were practiced, the Euro-Americans would disappear from the earth and the dead ancestors of the Indians would return to life along with the game, fish, and plants that had disappeared (Fowler and Liljeblad 1986:460).

2. Boas Collection, Archie Phinney correspondence, October 28, 1929. American Philosophical Society.

3. Ibid., November 20, 1929.

4. In the summer of 2006, one of the two passed away and is sorely missed.

Chapter Three (pages 69-93)

1. Blanchard 1983:115-30.
2. Tafoya 1989:29-41.
3. Bellah et al. 1991.
4. Labaree 1997:39-81.
5. Cuban 1990:8.
6. Center for Civic Education 1995.
7. Padilla 1990:15-25.
8. Banks 1991:135-40.
9. Labaree 1997:39-81.
10. Moses 2000:1-19.
11. Derrida 1998:30.
12. Tafoya 1989:29-41 and Philips 1972:370-94.
13. Adley-SantaMaria 1997:129-43 and Philips 1983.
14. Novick, Fisher and Ko 2000.
15. Philips 1983.
16. Pat Burk (Chief Policy Officer at the Office of the Oregon State Superintendent), Personal Communication, 2005.
17. Haynes 2004:87-102.
18. Blanchard 1983:115-30 and Cantoni 1997.
19. Moses 2000:10.
20. Equity Coalition for Race, Gender, and National Origin 1992.
21. Bougie, Wright and Taylor 2003:349-73.
22. Demmert 1994; Henry and Pepper 1990:85-94; Novick and Fisher 2002; Trujillo 1997:10-21; U.S. Department of Education Office of Educational Research and Improvement 1995.
23. Cantoni 1997:1-9.
24. Whorf 1941:3.
25. Kramsch 2003:235-61.
26. Haynes 2004:87-102.
27. Fishman 2001:3-4.
28. Haynes 2004:91.

29. Greymorning 1999:6.
30. Taylor 1994.
31. Blanchard 1983.
32. Reyhner and Tennant 1993.
33. Testimonies given to the Oregon Senate's Education Committee in favor of Senate Bill 690, March 8th, 2004.
34. Haynes 2004.
35. Ibid., 92.
36. Cuban 1990.
37. Bureau of Indian Affairs 2006. Available online: http://www.doi.gov/bureau-indian-affairs.html.
38. Indian Nations at Risk Task Force 1991:cover.
39. Ibid., 16.
40. The Oregon Teachers' Association lobbied for these provisions, which were not originally approved by the Senate Education Committee. Members of that committee argued that elders and language teachers should have the *option* to seek such assistance if they deemed it necessary, but that it was condescending to *require* it.
41. Haynes 2004.
42. McIntosh 1989.
43. Haynes 2004.
44. Oregon Department of Education 2004.
45. Ibid.
46. Ibid.
47. Baron 1990.
48. Hakuta 1990.
49. Duignan 1999.
50. Padilla 1990 and Tse 2001.
51. Baron 1990:180.
52. Ibid.
53. Brandt 1990:216.
54. Baron 1990.
55. Lewelling 1992.

Chapter Four (pages 94-116)

1. Cited in Hallowell 2002:14.
2. Task Force on Terminated and Nonfederally Recognized Indian Tribes, Hearing #10 Salem, Oregon, March 13, 1976.
3. See, for example, Robert Bieder's introductory discussion in *Science Encounters the Indian, 1820-1880,* 1986:8; Douglas Cole's preface to *Captured Heritage: The Scramble for Northwest Coast Artifacts,* 1985: ix; and Vine Deloria's essay "Evolutionary Prejudice" in *Red Earth, White Lies: Native Americans and the Myth of Scientific Fact,* 1995:49.
4. Mihesuah 2003:71.
5. Barringer and Flynn 1998; Bieder 1986; Cole 1985; Krech 1999; Thornton 1999.
6. Collins 1998: 256-70.
7. Bordewich 1996: 173-75.
8. Sapir 1921.
9. See, for example, the edited collections by Brush and Stabinsky 1996 and Greaves 1994.
10. Vine Deloria, Jr., has written extensively about this topic in his article "Anthropologists and other Friends" in *Custer Died for Your Sins,* 1969; *Red Earth, White Lies,* 1995; and "Anthros, Indians and Planetary Reality" in *Indians and Anthropologists,* 1997. See also Smith 1999 and Medicine 2001.
11. Deloria 1969; Smith 1999.
12. See, for example, Angela Cavender Wilson's discussion of white scholars not caring to engage Native Americans for their perspectives of their own history (Wilson 1998: 23-36).
13. Gmelch 1997:165-72.
14. Darcy McNickle wrote that anthropologists believed that Native people were disappearing and that this theory was still being used in government decision processes regarding the administration of Native American nations in 1962. Anthropological opinions still affect Native American tribes as we can see in the Native American Graves and Repatriation Act of 1990, which establishes that anthropologists' opinions may decide cultural ownership.
15. Medicine 2001.
16. Haley and Wilcoxon 1997
17. Phil Cash Cash is a member of the Confederated Tribes of Umatilla.
18. See http://www.leg.state.or.us/05orlaws/sess0001.dir/0098ses.htm

Chapter Five (pages 117-146)

1. Crawford 1998.
2. Chomsky 1957.
3. Hymes 1964.
4. Canale 1983.
5. Bills 1997.
6. Freire 2000:34.
7. Kirlin 2003.
8. Omaggio Hadley 2001.
9. Bruner 1983.
10. Gardner 1983.
11. Lee and VanPatten 2003:117-18.
12. Ibid., 121-23.
13. Ibid., 124-25.
14. Ibid., 126.
15. Ibid., 126-28.
16. Hinton 2002.
17. Linn et al. 2002.
18. American Council on the Teaching of Foreign Language 2005.
19. Bosch 1997:33-69.
20. Hudson 1999:121.
21. Lee and VanPatten 2003:126.
22. Houser and Toosarvandani 2006.
23. Barker 1981.
24. Bommelyn 1995.
25. Krashen 1982.
26. Crawford 2000.
27. Fishman 1991:19
28. Linn et al. 2002:115.
29. Ibid., 119.
30. Aitchison 1991:13.

Bibliography

When we have been able to find Web sites of the sources, we have included them; all sites were accessed in January 2007.

Adley-SantaMaria, Bernadette 1997 White Mountain Apache Language: Issues in Language Shift, Textbook Development, and Native Speaker-University Collaboration. In *Teaching Indigenous Languages*. Jon Reyhner, ed. Pp. 129-43. Flagstaff: Northern Arizona University Press.

Aitchison, Jean 1991 *Language Change: Progress or Decay?* 2nd edition. New York: Cambridge University Press.

American Council on the Teaching of Foreign Languages 2005 *Integrated Performance Assessment Manual.* New York: American Council on the Teaching of Foreign Languages.

Aoki, Haruo 1975 The East Plateau Linguistic Diffusion Area. *International Journal of American Linguistics* 41(3): 183-99.

Armstrong, Jerome Benjamin 2004 A Survey of Oregon's Endangered Native American Languages. M.A. Thesis, Portland State University.

Banks, James 1991 Multicultural Literacy and Curriculum Reform. *Education Horizons* 69(3):135-40.

Barker, M. A. R. 1981 *Klamath Grammar.* Berkeley: University of California Press.

Baron, Dennis 1990 *The English-Only Question: An Official Language for Americans?* New Haven: Yale University Press.

Barringer, Tim, and Tom Flynn. 1998 *Colonialism and the Object: Empire, Material Culture and the Museum.* London, England: Routledge.

Bellah, Robert et al. 1991 *The Good Society.* New York: Alfred A. Knopf.

Bieder, Robert 1986 *Science Encounters the Indian, 1820-1880: The Early Years of American Ethnology.* Norman: University of Oklahoma Press.

Bills, Garland 1997 Language shift, linguistic variation, and teaching Spanish to native speakers in the United States. In *La enseñanza del español a hispanohablantes: Práxis y teoría.* M. C. Colombi, and F. X. Alarcón, eds. Pp. 263-82. Boston, MA: Houghton Mifflin Company.

Blanchard, Evelyn Lance 1983 The Growth and Development of American Indian and Alaskan Native Children. In The Psychosocial Development of Minority Group Children. Gloria Johnson Powell, ed. Pp. 115-130. New York : Brunner/Mazel.

Bommelyn, Loren Me'lashne 1995 *Now You're Speaking Tolowa.* Arcata, CA: Center for Indian Community Development, Humboldt State University.

Bonnell, Sonciray 1997 Chemawa Indian Boarding School: The First One Hundred Years, 1880-1980. Ph.D. dissertation, Dartmouth College.

Bordewich, Fergus M. 1996 *Killing the White Man's Indian: Reinventing Native Americans at the End of the Twentieth Century.* Pp. 173-75. New York: Anchor Books.

Bosch, Laura, and Nuria Sebastian-Galles 1997 Native-language recognition abilities in 4-month-old infants from monolingual and bilingual environments. *Cognition* 65(1):33-69.

Bougie, Évelyne, Stephen Wright, and Donald Taylor 2003 Early Heritage Language Education and the Abrupt Shift to a Dominant-Language Classroom: Impact on the Personal and Collective Esteem of Inuit Children in Arctic Québec. *International Journal of Bilingual Education and Bilingualism* 6(5): 349-73.

Boyd, Robert 1999 *The Coming of the Spirit of Pestilence: Introduced Infectious Diseases and Population Decline among Northwest Coast Indians, 1774-1874*. Seattle; University of Washington Press.

Brandt, Elizabeth 1990 The Official English movement and the role of first languages. In *Perspectives on Official English: the Campaign for English as the Official Language of the USA*. Karen L. Adams and Daniel T. Brink, eds. Pp. 215-28. New York: Mouton de Gruyter.

Bruner, Jerome 1983 *Child's Talk: Learning to Use Language*. New York: W. W. Norton.

Brush, Stephen B., and Doreen Stabinsky, eds. 1996 *Valuing Local Knowledge: Indigenous Peoples and Intellectual Property Rights*. Washington, D.C.: Island Press.

Bureau of Indian Affairs 2006 Available online:http://www.doi.gov/bureau-indian-affairs.html

Canale, Michael 1983 From communicative competence to communicative language pedagogy. In *Language and Communication*. J. Richards and R. Schmidt, eds. London, England: Longman.

Cantoni, Gina 1997 Keeping minority languages alive: The school's responsibility. In *Teaching Indigenous Languages*. Jon Reyhner, ed. Flagstaff: Northern Arizona University.

Carney, Cary Michael 1999 *Native American Higher Education in the United States*. New Brunswick, N.J.: Transaction Publishers.

Cash Cash, Phil 2005 Sources for Chinook Jargon, a Pacific Northwest Pidgin. Available online: http://www.u.arizona.edu/~cashcash/CJ_sources_pcc.pdf.

Center for Civic Education 1995 The Role of Civic Education: A Report of the Task Force on Civic Education. The Second Annual White House Conference on Character Building for a Democratic, Civil Society. Calabasas, CA: Center for Civic Education.

Chomsky, Noam 1957 *Syntactic Structures*. The Hague, Netherlands: Mouton.

Cole, Douglas 1985 *Captured Heritage: The Scramble for Northwest Coast Artifacts*. Seattle: University of Washington Press.

Collins, James 1998 Our ideologies and theirs. In *Language Ideologies: Practice and Theory*. B. Schieffelin, K. Woolard, and P. Kroskrity, eds. Pp. 256-70. Oxford, England: Oxford University -Press.

Confederated Tribes of the Siletz Indians of Oregon 1984 The Tribal Comprehensive Plan Nesika-Alki (Our Future). Eagle Graphics and Associates.

Conklin, Nancy F., and Margaret A. Lourie 1983 *A Host of Tongues: Language Communities in the United States*. New York: Macmillan

Crawford, James 2000 At War with Diversity: U.S. Language Policy in an Age of Anxiety. Buffalo, NY: Multilingual Matters Ltd.

Cuban, Larry 1990 Reforming again, again, and again. *Educational Researcher*. Jan.-Feb.:8.

Deloria, Vine Jr.,
1969 *Custer Died for Your Sins*. New York: Macmillan.
1995 *Red Earth, White Lies*. New York: Scribner.
1997 Anthros, Indians and planetary reality. In *Indians and Anthropologists*. T. Biolsi, ed. Tucson: University of Arizona Press.

Demmert, William 1994 Blueprints for Indian education: Languages and cultures. *ERIC Digest*. Washington D.C.: ERIC Clearinghouse on Languages and Linguistics. Available online: http://www.ericdigests.org/1995-1/languages.htm

Denis, Armelle 2001 Using Computers for Reversing Language Shift: Ethical and Pragmatic Implications from Wasco Case Study. M.A. Thesis, Oregon State University.

Derrida, Jacques 1998 *Monolingualism of the Other or The Prosthesis of Origin.* Patrick Mensah, trsl. Stanford: Stanford University Press.

Dominica, Sister Mary 1959 *Willamette Interlude.* Palo Alto, CA: Pacific Books.

Duignan, Peter 1999 Bilingual education: A critique. *Hoover Essays* 22. Stanford, CA: The Hoover Institution on War, Revolution, and Peace.

Equity Coalition for Race, Gender, and National Origin 1992 *Programs for Equal Opportunity.* Michigan: University of Michigan School of Education.

Fishman, Joshua
1991 Reversing Language Shift: Theoretical and Empirical Foundations of Assistance to Threatened Languages. Philadelphia, PA: Multilingual Matters Ltd.
2001 Why is it so hard to save a threatened language? A perspective on the cases that follow. In *Can Threatened Languages Be Saved?* Pp. 1-22. New York: Multilingual Matters Ltd.

Fowler, Catherine, and Sven Liljeblad 1986 Northern Paiute. In *Handbook of North American Indians, Great Basin* vol. 11, W. D'Azevedo, ed. Washington D.C.: Smithsonian Institution.

Freire, Paulo 2000 *Pedagogy of the Oppressed.* 30th anniversary edition. New York: Continuum.

Gardner, Howard 1983 *Frames of Mind: The Theory of Multiple Intelligences.* New York: Basic Books.

Gibbs, George 1863 *A Dictionary of the Chinook Jargon or Trade Language of Oregon.* Washington, D.C.: Smithsonian Institution.

Gmelch, George 1997 Of softball bats and fishnets: A summer in the Alaskan bush. In *The Naked Anthropologist: Tales from Around the World.* P. Devita, ed. Pp. 165-72. Belmont, CA: Wadsworth Publishing Company.

Greaves, Thomas (ed.) 1994 *Intellectual Property Rights for Indigenous Peoples: A Sourcebook.* Oklahoma City: Society for Applied Anthropology.

Greymorning, Stephen 1999 Running the gauntlet of an indigenous language program. In *Revitalizing Indigenous Language.* J. Reyhner, ed. Pp. 6-16. Flagstaff: Northern Arizona University Press. Avaliable online: http://jan.ucc.nau.edu/~jar/RIL_2.html

Hajda, Yvonne, Henry Zenk, and Robert Boyd 1988 The early historiography of Chinook Jargon. Paper presented at the 87th Annual Meeting of the American Anthropological Association.

Hakuta, Kenji 1990 Language and cognition in bilingual children. In *Bilingual Education: Issues and Strategies.* A. M. Padilla, H. H. Fairchild, and C. M. Valdez, eds. Pp. 47-59. Newbury Park, CA: Corwin Press, Inc. Available online: http://www.stanford.edu/~hakuta/www/research/publications/(1990)%20-%20LANGUAGE%20AND%20COGNITION%20IN%20BILINGUAL%20CHILDREN.pdf

Hale, Horatio 1890 *An International Idiom: A Manual of the Oregon Trade Language, or 'Chinook Jargon.'* London, England: Whittaker.

Haley, Brian, and Larry Wilcoxon 1997 Anthropology and the making of Chumash tradition. *Current Anthropology* 38(5):761-94.

Hall, Roberta 1978 Oral Traditions of the Coquille Indians. Oregon State University.

Hallowell, A. Irving 2002 Introduction. In *American Anthropology 1888-1920: Papers from the American Anthropologist.* F. de Laguna, ed. Lincoln: University of Nebraska Press.

Harrison, J. B. 1887 *The Latest Studies on Indian Reservations.* Philadelphia, PA: Indian Rights Association.

Haynes, Erin 2004 Obstacles facing tribal language programs in Warm Springs, Klamath, and Grand Ronde. *Coyote Papers* 13:87-102. Available online: http://coyotepapers.sbs.arizona.edu/CPXIII/haynes.pdf

Hendricks, Robert 1937 *Innnnnnng Haaaaaaa! A Trilogy in the Anabasis of the West.* n.p. Salem, OR.

Henry, Steven L., and Floy C. Pepper 1990 Cognitive, social, and cultural effects on Indian learning style: Classroom implications. *The Journal of Educational Issues of Language Minority Students*, 7 (Special Issue): 85-94.

Hinton, Leanne 2002 *How to Keep Your Language Alive: A Commonsense Approach to One-on-One Language Learning.* Berkeley, CA: Heyday Books.

Houser, Michael J., and Maziar Toosarvandani 2006 Nonsyntactic ordering effects in syntactic noun incorporation. Symposium conducted at the 2006 annual meeting of the Linguistic Society of America, January, Albuquerque NM.

Hudson, Gover 1999 *Essential Introductory Linguistics.* Oxford, England: Blackwell Publishing.

Hudson, John 1993 A Kalapuya prophecy. In *From Here We Speak: An Anthology of Oregon Poetry*. I. Wendt and P. St. John, eds. Dell Hymes, trsl. P. 30. Corvallis: Oregon State University Press.

Hymes, Dell, ed. 1964 *Language in Culture and Society.* New York: Harper and Row.

Hymes, Dell

1980 Commentary. In *Theoretical Orientations in Creole Studies*. A. Valdman and A. Highfield, eds. Pp. 389-423. New York: Academic Press.

2007 Languages and their uses. In *The First Oregonians*, second edition, Laura Berg, ed. Portland: Oregon Council for the Humanities.

Indian Nations at Risk Task Force 1991 Indian nations at risk: An educational strategy for action (Final report of the Indian Nations at Risk Task Force). Washington, D.C.: U.S. Department of Education.

Jackson, Helen 1993 *A Century of Dishonor.* New York: Indian Head Books.

Kip, Lawrence 1855 Indian Council in the Valley of the Walla Walla. Available online: http://www.ccrh.org/comm/river/treaties/kipp.htm

Kirlin, Mary 2003 The Role of Civic Skills in Fostering Civic Engagement Circle Working Paper 06. Available online http://civicyouth.org/PopUps/WorkingPapers/WP06Kirlin.pdf

Kramsch, Claire 2003 Language, thought, and culture. In *The Handbook of Applied Linguistics*. A. Davies and C. Elder, eds. Pp. 235-61. Boston, MA: Blackwell.

Krashen, Stephen 1982 Principles and Practice in Second Language Acquisition. New York: Pergamon Press.

Krech, Shepard, III 1999 *Collecting Native America, 1870-1960.* Washington, D.C.: Smithsonian Institution.

Labaree, D. F. 1997 Public goods, private goods: The American struggle over educational goals. *American Educational Research Journal* 34(1), 39-81.

Lee, James, and Bill VanPatten 2003 *Making Communicative Language Teaching Happen.* 2nd edition. Pp. 117-18. Boston, MA: McGraw-Hill.

Lemmon, Burton C. The Historical Development of the Chemawa Indian School. M.S. Thesis, Oregon State College 1941, p. 26.

Lewelling, Vickie W. 1992 English plus. *ERIC Digest*. Washington D.C.: ERIC Clearinghouse on Languages and Linguistics. Available online: http://eric.ed.gov/ERICDocs/data/ericdocs2/content_storage_01/0000000b/80/2a/1d/27.pdf

Lewis, David 2002 Native experience and perspectives from correspondence in the SWORP Archive. In *Changing Landscapes: Sustaining Traditions*, proceedings of the 5th and 6th annual Coquille Cultural Preservation Conferences. North Bend, OR: Coquille Indian Tribe.

Linn, Mary S., et al. 2002 Awakening the languages: Challenges of enduring language programs: Field reports from 15 programs from Arizona, New Mexico and Oklahoma. In *Indigenous Languages across the Community.* B. Burnaby and J. Rehyner, eds. Flagstaff: College of Education, Northern Arizona University. Available online: http://jan.ucc.nau.edu/~jar/ILAC/ILAC_13.pdf

McIntosh, Peggy 1989 White privilege: Unpacking the invisible knapsack. *Peace and Freedom* July/August. Available online: http://seamonkey.ed.asu.edu/~mcisaac/emc598ge/Unpacking.html

McNickle, D'Arcy 1962 *The Indian Tribes of the United States: Ethnic and Cultural Survival.* Oxford Institute of Race Relations.

Mechelli, Andrea, et al. 2004 Neurolinguistics: Structural plasticity in the bilingual brain. *Nature,* October 431(7010):757. Available online:http://www.nature.com/nature/journal/v431/n7010/full/431757a.html

Medicine, Beatrice 2001 *Learning to be an Anthropologist and Remaining "Native," Selected Writings.* Champaign, IL: University of Illinois Press.

Mihesuah, Devon A. 2003 *Indigenous American Women: Decolonization, Empowerment, Activism.* P. 71. Lincoln: University of Nebraska Press.

Moses, Michele 2000 Why bilingual education policy is needed: A philosophical response to the critics. *Bilingual Research Journal* 24(4):1-19. Available online: http://brj.asu.edu/v244/abstractt.html

Novick, Rebecca, Amy Fisher, and Lena Ko 2000 [1983] *The Unity Project: Creating a Circle of Awareness.* Portland, OR: Northwest Regional Educational Laboratory.

Novick, Rebecca, and Amy Fisher 2002 *Sharing the Wisdom of Practice: Schools that Optimize Literacy Learning for All Children.* Portland, OR: Northwest Regional Educational Laboratory.

Omaggio Hadley, Alice 2001 *Teaching Language in Context*, 3rd edition. Boston, MA: Heinle & Heinle.

Oregon Department of Education 2004 *Oregon Public Charter School Handbook.* 3rd edition. Salem: Oregon Department of Education.

Padilla, Amado 1990 Bilingual education: Issues and perspectives. In *Bilingual Education: Issues and Strategies.* A. M. Padilla, H. H. Fairchild, and C. M. Valdez, eds. Pp. 15-25. Newbury Park, CA: Corwin Press.

Philips, Susan
1972 Participant structures and communicative competence: Warm Springs children in community and classroom. In *Functions of Language in the Classroom.* C. Cazden, V. P. John, and D. Hymes, eds. Pp. 370-94. New York: Teachers College Press.
1983 *The Invisible Culture: Communication in Classroom and Community on the Warm Springs Indian Reservation.* Prospect Heights, IL: Waveland Press.

Reddick, SuAnn, and Cary Collins 2005 Medicine Creek to Fox Island: Cadastral scams and contested domains. *Oregon Historical Quarterly,* Fall. Available online: http://www.historycooperative.org/journals/ohq/106.3/reddick.html#REF51

Reyhner, Jon, and Edward Tennant 1993 Maintaining and Renewing Native Languages. In *Heritage Languages in America.* Washington, D.C.:Center for Applied Linguistics. Available online: http://www.cal.org/heritage/resources/art_maintaining.html

Reyhner, Jon, and Jeanne Eder 2004 *American Indian Education: A History.* Norman: University of Oklahoma Press.

Riebe, Naomi 1976 Task Force on Terminated and Nonfederally Recognized Indian Tribes, Transcription of Hearing #10, Salem, Oregon, March 13, 1976. Seattle: National Archives and Records Administration, Pacific Northwest Region.

Ryan, W. Carson 1931 Federal-state cooperation in Indian education. *School and Society* September 26, 34(874):418-26.

Samarin, William 1996 Arctic origin and domestic development of Chinook Jargon. In *Language Contact in the Arctic: Northern Pidgins and Contact Languages.* E. Jahr and I. Broch, eds. Pp. 321-39. New York: Mouton de Gruyter.

Sapir, Edward 1921 *Language.* New York: Harcourt Brace Jovanavich.

Smith, Linda Tuhwai 1999 *Decolonizing Methodologies.* New York: Zed Books.

Tafoya, Terry 1989 Coyote's eyes: Native cognition styles. *Journal of American Indian Education.* August (Special Issue):29-41.

Taylor, Charles 1994 The politics of recognition. In *Multiculturalism: Examining the Politics of Recognition.* A. Gutman, ed. Pp. 25-73. Princeton, NJ: Princeton University Press.

Thomason, Sarah G. 1983 Chinook Jargon in areal and historical context. *Language* 59:820-70.

Thornton, Russell 1999 *Studying Native America: Problems and Prospects.* Madison: University of Wisconsin Press.

Trujillo, Octaviana 1997 A tribal approach to language and literacy development in a trilingual setting. In *Teaching Indigenous Languages.* J. Reyhner, ed. Pp. 10-21. Flagstaff: Northern Arizona University.

Tse, Lucy 2001 *Why Don't They Learn English?: Separating Fact from Fallacy in the U.S. Language Debate.* New York: Teachers College Press.

U.S. Congress
1859 Senate, 36th Congress, First Session, Serial 1023. Ex. Doc. No. 192 letter from R. B. Metcalfe, Indian Agent, Siletz Indian Agency to Edward R. Geary, Esq., Superintendent of Indian Affairs (Salem), July 8.
1863 House of Representatives, 38th Congress, First Session, Serial. Ex. Doc. No. 1. 1182, No. 4. Pp. 178-81; No. 23. Pp. 202-4. Washington, D.C.: Government Printing Office.

U.S. Department of Education, Office of Educational Research and Improvement 1995 Promising Programs in Native Education. Regional Educational Laboratory Network.

Whorf, Benjamin 1941 The relation of habitual thought and behavior to language. In *Language, Culture and Personality: Essays in Memory of Edward Sapir.* Leslie Spier, ed. Pp. 75-93. Menasha, WI: Sapir Memorial Publication Fund. Available online: http://sloan.stanford.edu/mousesite/Secondary/Whorfframe2.html

Wilson, Angela Cavender 1998 American Indian history or non-Indian perceptions of American Indian history. In *Natives and Academics: Researching and Writing about American Indians.* D. Mihesuah, ed. Lincoln: University of Nebraska Press.

Archival Collections Used

University of Oregon Libraries, Special Collections, Southwest Oregon Research Project 268, Series 1 & 2, Record Group 75, National Archives and Records Administration, Washington, D.C.

American Philosophical Society, Boas Collection, Correspondence with Leo Frachtenberg, Melville Jacobs, and Archie Phinney.

Online Sources

Web sources are ever-growing. To read about Oregon's tribes from their own perspective check out the tribal webpages below:

Burns Paiute Tribe: http://www.burnspaiute-nsn.gov/TheTribe.htm
Coos, Lower Umpqua, Siuslaw Tribe: http://216.128.13.185/CTCLUSINEW/
Culture/CultureHistory/tabid/228/Default.aspx
Coquille Tribe: http://www.cedco.net/tribe.shtml
Cow Creek Band: http://www.cowcreek.com/story/index.html
Grand Ronde: http://www.grandronde.org/culture/
Klamath Tribe: http://www.klamathtribes.org/history.html
Siletz Tribe: http://ctsi.nsn.us/History_and_Culture.html
Umatilla Tribe: http://www.umatilla.nsn.us/history.html
Warm Springs: http://www.warmsprings.com/Warmsprings/Tribal_
Community/History__Culture/

Here are some other websites with information on Oregon Native languages:

Bureau of Indian Affairs: http://www.doi.gov/bureau-indian-affairs.html
Don Mcnaughtan's American Indians: http://www.lanecc.edu/library/don/
indexsite.htm
Ethnologue: http://www.ethnologue.com/web.asp
Library of Congress: http://international.loc.gov/intldl/find/digital_collections.
html
The Linguist List: http://linguistlist.org/
Native Languages of the Americas: http://www.native-languages.org
Northwest Digital Archives: http://nwda.wsulibs.wsu.edu/
Northwest Indian Language Institute: http://babel.uoregon.edu/nili/
Scott Delancey's Klamath-Modoc Linguistics Page: http://www.uoregon.
edu/~delancey/klamath.html
Scott Delancey's Penutian Linguistics Page: http://www.uoregon.edu/
~delancey/penutian.html
Southern Oregon Digital Archives: http://soda.sou.edu/
Southwest Oregon Research Project: http://gladstone.uoregon.edu/~coyotez/
University of Washington, Kalapuya Texts: http://www.lib.washington.edu/
types/texts/K.html
Phil Cash Cash's Web site: http://www.u.arizona.edu/~cashcash/
Teaching Indigenous Languages: http://jan.ucc.nau.edu/~jar/TIL.html
Yamada Language Center Font Archive: http://babel.uoregon.edu/yamada/
fonts.html

166